Approaching Neverland

A Memoir of Epic Tragedy & Happily Ever After

Peggy Kennedy

iUniverse, Inc.
New York   Bloomington

Approaching Neverland
A Memoir of Epic Tragedy & Happily Ever After

iUniverse books may be ordered through booksellers or by contacting:

iUniverse
1663 Liberty Drive
Bloomington, IN 47403
www.iuniverse.com
1-800-Authors (1-800-288-4677)

ISBN: 978-1-4401-2613-0 (pbk)
ISBN: 978-1-4401-2612-3 (cloth)
ISBN: 978-1-4401-2614-7 (ebk)

Library of Congress Control Number: 2009923111

Printed in the United States of America

iUniverse rev. date:3/23/2009

For Shane and Blake

Acknowledgments

I would like to thank Denis Ledoux, for helping me start this book, and Adair Lara, for helping me finish it; Auntie Sissy, Vera Dickie, and cousins Jackie and Mary for generously providing perspective, dates, and memories; the friends who cheered me on no matter how many times I had to tell them the book was not quite done; Eileen Williams, sister and sounding board extraordinaire; Mom, Dad, Glenn, and Joan, for their eternal inspiration; sister Sue, who told me to write from my passion, and brother Patrick, whose passion for this book kept me going; Shane and Blake, who stayed eager to read it; and Paul, who made it all possible.

Prologue

Who's that knocking on the door?

Oh good—it's you!

Grab a tissue and some coffee; cups are laid out on the counter.

Sit down in the burnt orange chair and gird your sides for laughter.

Dad will light a fire, and we'll all settle in.

Do you mind if Mom smokes?

The story's been held too close for way too long.

But they told me I could tell it now.

So let's jump right in ...

Part I

Sink or Swim

1960

Chapter 1

🌿❧

Cannonball

September, 1960

"Up and at 'em, girls, we're running a little late." My father's wingtips thumped down the stairs as he yelled upward. My heart raced. It was the first day of school. I was five years old.

My older sisters Joan, eight, and Sue, nine, were already getting dressed. I hurried to the closet, yanked my uniform off its hanger and imitated Joan—button blouse, jumper over her head, fold-over white socks—then shoved my feet in my shoes and stumbled after her down to the kitchen. Usually my mother would already be there in her fluffy pink bathrobe, stirring a hefty spoonful of sugar into her coffee and getting Kilpatrick's bread out of the cupboard for our lunches. You entered our kitchen through a louvered swing door. There was a chrome table and matching chairs with gray and white swirled plastic cushions that

3

my mother's mother had passed on to us. The linoleum floor, a zigzag of maroon, green, and beige, was kept in place with a metal trim. Daddy noticed my looking around. "She's tired this morning," he said. "She needs her rest." I stared miserably into the bowl as I ate my Cheerios. All the other mommies would be driving their first graders today.

St. Louis Bertrand's School was on 100th Avenue at East 14th St. in Oakland, a beige bread box of a building next to the St. Louis Bertrand Church. Patrick pulled me through the empty hall to my class and then stopped me before he let me go in. "Hold on, Peg." He whisked a comb from his pocket and ran it roughly through my ponytail. Then the bell rang, and he dashed off.

The nun, in a white gown and white hood to her waist, nodded when I entered. The white band around her face made her look as if she didn't have any hair or ears. I sat down and folded my hands as Pat had instructed me to do. Marie Johnson, my best friend, whose black skin was so different from mine, sat two rows over. Her hair was braided with colorful beads. She bent forward over her desk to get my attention, and we exchanged smiles and little waves. Timmy Bertelson, whose father had the butcher shop where Mom let me get a piece of bologna while she shopped, was three seats behind her. Michael Maloney, the kindergarten troublemaker, was next to me.

The nun strode through the rows of desks, rosary beads swishing at her side. When she stopped at my desk, my heart pounded. I smiled meekly.

"Young lady, please come with me," she said. As I followed her to her desk at the front of the class, I felt my collar to make sure it hadn't gotten twisted, as Joan's sometimes did, and checked my uniform and shoes: everything seemed okay. Maybe, I thought hopefully, she liked how I had been sitting so nicely and was going to give me a holy card. Sue and Joan both had collections of holy cards they had earned in class. I had long looked forward to getting my first one.

"What is your name?" she asked.

"Peggy Kennedy, Sister," I answered.

"Miss Kennedy, please stand here by my desk for a moment." She stepped out into the hallway.

Michael Maloney whispered, "You're gonna get in trouble!" and some of the children laughed. I was comforted to notice that Marie didn't. I felt my face heat up and willed myself fruitlessly not to blush.

The teacher came back with Father Hecht. I recognized him from Sunday Mass. He was large, filling out every inch of his long black robe.

"Keep your thoughts to yourself," Sister advised Michael Maloney, to my delight. "I am Sister Augustine Mary," she told the class. She had written the name on the board and told us we should practice writing it as we would be writing it on our papers all year. She said she'd be gone for the next few minutes, and that Father Hecht would help them while she was gone.

Sister took me firmly by the hand and led me down the empty hallway to the girl's bathroom. There, she turned me to face the mirror. Mom had cut my bangs shorter than usual—they barely grazed the top of my forehead, and sometimes I tugged on them as if that would make them grow back faster. I tried to straighten my glasses. They were always slipping down and never seemed to sit straight on my nose. Maybe Joan was right: my ears were too crooked for glasses to hang right on them. The year before, my right eye had started to cross, throwing off my depth perception. When I began bumping into walls and then fell down the stairs, my parents took me to the eye doctor. The doctor recommended surgery, but Mom and Dad couldn't afford it. They took the alternative approach: a pair of thick eyeglasses. I chose pink ones with pointed corners. Although I liked seeing where I was going, I hated looking different than my siblings.

"Miss Kennedy, did your mother brush your hair this morning?" Sister Augustine asked, kindly. In class, she had seemed hardhearted, but here with just the two of us, her blue eyes looked soft.

"No, Sister." I stared at the yellowish linoleum, my face burning with shame.

"I'm going to brush the back of your hair to get the knots out." She pulled a small brush from a hidden pocket in her robe. I steeled my head and shoulders for the yanking to come. Instead, she brushed my hair as my mother did, working through it gently, holding my head in place with one hand while almost tenderly brushing through the knots with the other. She was done a few minutes later.

"That's better," she said. She turned me so that I could see the back of my hair in the mirror. I had never seen the back of my hair before, but I nodded anyway. When she smiled, I realized that she was younger than I had thought: she didn't look any older than my Cousin Jackie. I smiled back.

"If your mommy forgets to brush your hair tomorrow before school, just remind her. I'm sure she just forgot this morning."

I nodded again and felt tears well up. I thought they'd spill over like the water in Uncle Jack's pool when he did his cannonball. The sister's kindness made me want to say, "My mommy's sick, and they might take her away." But Glenn and Pat had warned me not to say anything to anyone about Mom. The water in the pool started to calm: I would not cry. I wiped the tears behind my glasses and rubbed my hands on my jumper.

"Are you okay?" Sister bent down to look at me with her hand on my shoulder. I nodded. As we walked back to class, her grip on my hand was much lighter. So this is first grade. I vowed to pay attention when my sisters brushed their hair the next morning. Surely it was something somebody already in first grade could learn to do.

* * *

We had a pink Tudor-style house on 108th Avenue with a steep roof and postage-stamp lawn that slightly sloped down to the sidewalk and a telephone pole. When it came time to replace the roof, Mom chose a pink one. Our black cocker spaniel Pogo's stub of a tail wagged as we girls walked through the front door from that first day of real school, clutching bags of candy bought on the way home; but that's where normal stopped. The breakfast dishes and milk were still on the table. The floor was strewn with clothes in piles. Mom wasn't fastidious, but things were usually put away. The three of us instinctively drew closer together in the kitchen. The refrigerator hummed comfortingly, but the chirp of a bird outside the half-opened kitchen window made me jump.

"Girls, is that you?" Mom called from upstairs, her voice high and squeaky like a child's. "Come here—I have something to show you!" Sue and Joan exchanged wary glances and walked up the stairs. I followed their steps close behind.

Mom was wearing a seersucker sun suit with ties at the shoulders. Her feet were bare. Her uncombed hair stuck out in unruly wisps like snakes. She stood inside a circle of objects next to her unmade bed: a statue of the Virgin Mary from our dining room credenza, her hairbrush, a rhinestone necklace, Glenn's record player, and a pair of my father's wingtips. The bench to her dresser table had fallen over, and drawers were pulled open, displaying her bras, underwear, and a padded pink jewelry box. We stared. Mom giggled. "I've been having the most fun today!" she said breathlessly. She placed the needle on one of Glenn's yellow 45 rpm records. The Lone Ranger blared. Mom trotted around her collection of objects, her head thrown back like an Indian circling a captured village.

"Mom, what are you doing?" Sue, her voice quaking, shouted over the music.

"Well, *Igatheredtogetherallmyfavoritethings,andI'vebeensittingh ereadmiring them*," Mom said so quickly that I barely understood her. When her Indian self started to visit, she always talked faster. Frightened, Joan and I were silent.

Sue made her voice quiet. "Mom, how about if we just put all these things back where they were?" Sue scooped up the statue of the Virgin Mary and Daddy's shoes. Joan picked up the brush and was going for the necklace when Mom yelled.

"*Don'ttouchthosethings!*" Mom grabbed Sue's arm and yanked her down in the middle of the circle. Mom always seemed to pick on Sue when she went crazy.

"Be careful, Mom: you don't want to hurt her. " Patrick had shown up at the door. He walked over and pried Mom's fingers from Sue's arm. Sue's lips crumpled, but she didn't cry. Mom stood up as if nothing had happened, walked into the bathroom and closed the door.

"I'll call Daddy," Glenn said. He had come in behind Patrick. My oldest brother Glenn had dark blue almond-shaped eyes that crinkled almost to nothing when he laughed. His eyebrows were so bushy that one of his high school friends said they looked like two caterpillars running to meet each other. The big bunny rabbit front teeth he had in common with the rest of us were slightly crossed until he got braces at fourteen.

In the morning everything seemed to be fine again. We continued to outward appearances normal. It was what the world required.

* * *

Mom and Dad had met as kids, when both of their mothers volunteered at St. Elizabeth's Catholic Church on 34th Avenue in the Fruitvale district of Oakland. They raced around folded tables and chairs in St Elizabeth's Community Hall as their mothers, dressed in flowered hats and fox stoles and hawking quilted cozies and crocheted baby blankets, turned a blind eye. Mom was intense and beautiful and shy, and Dad was sweetly mischievous. Dad was a junior in high school, and Mom was a sophomore when she began watching him play outfield, sending the ball to the catcher in a long arc. She knew Dad thought tennis boring, so when he came to watch her play in a school tournament one day, sitting forward in the bleachers in his baseball cap, she knew he liked her, too. She blew her serve, knowing he was watching. It wasn't long before you never saw one without the other.

My father enlisted in World War II after high school in 1942, right after he turned seventeen. He joined the 82nd Airborne, a parachute infantry regiment. In her senior year, Mom got a job in Capwell's Department Store's gift wrap department; she prided herself on cutting just the right amount of paper to fit a box and using scotch tape sparingly. (Giving gifts made her giddy—so much so that she couldn't keep our Christmas presents a secret. She would sneak us into her closet to show us our other siblings' gifts so we'd know exactly what we were getting. She gave us all the same robes and pajamas and slippers, only in different colors—I always got pink. The wrappings were brilliantly creased and the stick-on bows perfectly off-center.) It was understood she and my father would get married when he got back. She bought a cedar chest and filled it with dishes and towels and a negligee for her wedding night. But the war dragged on. Dad was good about writing, but still there were months when no letters came. My mother scoured the papers for news and listened anxiously to President Roosevelt's weekly radio fireside chats, her face pinched and nervous.

In the months before Christmas in 1944, after hearing reports of heavy casualties in Belgium, where my father was stationed, she began to skip work to stay glued to the radio. Capwell's fired her. After that, she hardly left the radio in her room. When she stopped coming down for dinner, her mother yelled through the door: "Barbara! Open the door! You need to get on with your life until Jack gets home or you'll get sick." Mom refused to unlock it. In any other family her mother might have meant she'd come down with a flu. But her mother was referring to a different kind of sickness.

Over the next few days, my mother cried often and ate little. The only thing that buoyed her spirits was playing the Glenn Miller album she and Daddy had danced to at his senior prom. Then on December 14, 1944, Glenn Miller was flying from England with his band to perform for the Allied troops in Paris when ice in the engine caused his plane to plunge into the English Channel. After that, things got muddled in my mother's mind. "Everyone must take cover," she heard the radio announcer say one day. "The Germans are attacking San Francisco." A plane flew over, and she heard bombs explode. She ran down the stairs and into the kitchen where her parents were eating oatmeal. Her mother was small with stocky legs and a large bosom usually covered with a belted, flower-print dress. "Barbara, for God's sakes," her mother said, "you look like a wild animal!" My grandfather looked up from his paper with dread. My mother had a raincoat thrown over her nightgown. Her hair was a matted clump, her eyes frantic in a face he didn't recognize, no doubt seeing for the first time in his daughter symptoms of the mental disorder he had secretly suffered through for years with his wife.

Although no one had ever told Mom about her mother's illness, she remembered her mother acting strange sometimes— her animated conversations with an empty chair or ransacking cupboards in search of some spice Mom had never heard of. But when she brought it up with her father, he told her she was imagining things. Once she'd heard her Dad mutter "Schizophrenia, Father" under his breath to their priest after Mass during one of her mother's long absences—described simply as restful respites from the children. But her mother never seemed rested when she came home. She'd been silent and withdrawn.

My mother was committed to Agnews Insane Asylum for the first time in 1945 when she was nineteen. Like all people with mental illness at that time, she was a guinea pig. Treatments were crude: shrieking, babbling, and thrashing patients were lashed to their beds with thick leather straps while others were pumped full of sedatives, left in rocking chairs to hum themselves lullabies, rolling back and forth for hours.

As my grandfather filled out the paperwork for her admission, my mother stood near enough to clutch at his sleeve, frightened by the stench of industrial cleanser and the muffled moans echoing along the corridors. She'd been his favorite, his companion on trips to the hardware store and lumber yard. They'd been a team. As he turned to leave, she threw herself on him in terror. "I'll be fine if I can just go home with you, Daddy!" My mother's eyes went flat as she repeated what her father said as he pulled his fedora down low over his eyes as they took her away: "Do everything they tell you, Barb, and you'll be okay."

She was there for six months. She was released shortly before Daddy returned home from the war. My grandfather had sent him a letter, telling him she'd been hospitalized for "nervousness." The letter scared Daddy—he knew about "nervousness" and what happened to people in the "loony bin"—but he never backed away. A lot of guys planned to break up with their girlfriends when they got home, but he wasn't one of them. The dream of starting a family with my mother had carried him through his darkest moments. How could he leave her now when she really needed him?

Daddy had his own phantoms when he returned and perhaps needed someone to stick with him, too. My mother told me that sometimes she'd catch him staring at nothing, his eyes pooling up with tears. He'd lost close friends, some from unopened parachutes; some shot and killed before they even touched the ground. He buried them deep inside himself. I wonder now if the migraine headaches he suffered from over the years were those friends come back to life, fighting and dying in Daddy's head.

Just weeks before coming home, my father helped to liberate a concentration camp. He walked, stunned, with the other American soldiers through the camp surrounded by barbed-wire fences, the hollow floors creaking under their boots. The smell of death led them to hundreds of emaciated corpses stacked like firewood. General Eisenhower had given the word to bury all of the bodies with a fitting service. Just two years before, Jack Kennedy, now barely twenty, had been scooping up easy grounders and firing the ball to first base, and slow dancing with my mother to Glenn Miller under crepe-paper and colored lights at a prom. Now, along with the rest of his regiment and American soldiers assigned to liberate camps throughout Europe, he dug graves and filled them, saying prayers for people he never knew, placing the Star of David and the occasional cross over each mound of soft earth. When he got back his black curly hair had gone straight and was flecked with gray; his mischievous looks had given way to teary stares and long stretches of silent, tortured remembering.

He enrolled in the police academy—lots of Irish guys from his old neighborhood in Oakland were becoming cops—but after a year of issuing tickets and breaking up fights, knew it wasn't for him. When his oldest sister Betty's fireman husband, Russ, invited him to try out, it made sense: my father wanted to save people, not arrest them. On May 10, 1947, not long after he traded his badge and gun in for an axe and a helmet and the day after Dad turned twenty-one, Mom and Dad got married. On February 11, 1948, nine months and two days later, my brother Glenn was born. Mom's mother put up a fuss that Mom named him after a bandleader instead of a saint, but Glenn Miller's music had brought Mom some happiness, and she wasn't about to change her mind. Mom, a good Catholic, had wanted ten children. Daddy, with a sure-footed grip on provisional economics, got a vasectomy after five. All of us were born on Breed Avenue.

One Sunday not long after school started we drove to church as usual in our beige four-door 1956 Ford station wagon. It had red upholstery with silver threads that scratched your legs and three bench seats. "Mom, I forgot my veil," Sue blurted as we pulled into the parking lot of St. Louis Bertrand's Church. Sue's curled brown hair framed her oval face. Her pointed white shoes were worldly next to my shiny black Mary Janes. I liked dressing up so much that I changed my clothes four or five times a day, sometimes shorts over a petty coat or pink Capri pants under a skirt. I now took pride in grooming and insisted on putting on my Mary Janes whenever I could get away with it. Mom was wearing a red hat shaped like a platter and red earrings. She opened the glove box, took out a black lump, and shook it out. "Here, honey, it's a little wrinkled, but it'll work." It was a round black lace veil that Mom kept in the glove box in case we forgot hats for church. We always wore veils to church except at Easter, when hats were worn with matching dresses and later Sue, Joan, and I would pose on our front lawn in front of Glenn and Patrick in matching outfits with Mom and Dad in back. Our family was big on holidays. There was a large cardboard pastel bunny taped to the inside of the window. In the photos I was always petticoat front and center.

We followed Mom's red heels to a pew near the middle of the church. Glenn slid in first, followed by Pat, Sue, Joan, me, and then Mom and Dad. Once we were seated, Mom licked her hankie and wiped my cheek. The sour smell of smoke spittle and holy water made my nose wrinkle.

It was a modern church, angular, with walls white and plain. Three stairs in a half circle lead to the altar. Other churches had gloriously vivid scenes on their windows, but St. Louis Bertrand's austerely contented itself with black line drawings on yellow glass depicting the Crucifixion like an unapproachable coloring book.

We all stood when Monsignor Brown walked up the center aisle swinging the incense ball, followed by Father Hecht and the altar boys. I liked listening to the choir sing while the organ played. Mom and Dad listened intently. I watched everyone else to see when to stand, kneel, and sit and made noises called "Latin."

Like Grandma, my father's mother, Monsignor Brown was from Ireland, but he was a lot harder to understand, so our attention wandered. The kids began whispering and giggling as they sent a message down the line. Glenn whispered to Patrick.

Pat to Sue, everyone turning so Mom couldn't see. But when Sue leaned in toward Joan, Mom caught her at it and frowned. Sue and Joan looked straight ahead, but then couldn't stand the suspense. Joan socked Sue in the arm in an attempt to beat the information out of her, so Sue whispered the message: "This *peee eeew* is full today."

Had she been anywhere else, Joan would have fallen to the ground in uncontrolled laughter. But now she managed to keep her legs and lower body still while her shoulders shook violently in silent glee. My mother glanced icily at Joan and Sue as if she didn't know them. Had that Indian crept inside Mom when I wasn't looking? I pinched her, hoping it would scare it away.

"Ow!" Mom screeched in a whisper close to my face. Her lips and eyes were mean. She slapped my hand. She had never done that before.

Monsignor Brown boomed from the lectern, "A reading from St. Luke, Chapter XV, page 693." Mom grabbed a missal. Tears burned my eyes. I scooted closer so I could pretend I was reading with her.

"And He spake this parable unto them, saying 'What man of you, having a hundred sheep, if he lose one of them, doth not leave the ninety and nine in the wilderness, and go after that which is lost, until he find it?'"

"'And when he hath found it,'" the priest continued, "'he layeth it on his shoulders, rejoicing.'"

I sighed as I leaned back against the pew. I liked this gospel. The lost sheep reminded me of Mom when her eyes did the two-step and she fancied herself an Indian. As far back as I could remember, Mom loved to play imaginary games. She'd march us around the house, until I felt my legs becoming spongy and imagined my toes growing claws as Mom's raspy voice sang us on the trail to a teddy bear's picnic. She brought tiny teacups filled with water and sat with me and my dolls on the rug and chatted about magical places we'd go. But sometimes when she pretended, she believed too much. Once, when I was four, Mom told us we were cowboys and to hide and she would be an Indian and try to find us. Giggling as I ran from the kitchen with the rest, I hid with Pat behind the dining room door while Joan, Sue, and Glenn hunkered down behind the couch. My mother's clothes and hair were the same, but when she found us, her face seemed tauter than it had been just minutes before as her lips seemed to stretch across her teeth in a smile. Her laugh was different too. Unlike her usual laugh, which shook her belly and shoulders and twinkled her eyes, this Indian laugh was high pitched while her body stood still. The only things that moved were her darting eyes.

It was not only the incense smoke that stuck to our clothing and followed us into the car that Sunday morning. The ominous sense of a change in our mother, one we were all too familiar with, came too. We kids kept silent; so the only sound inside the car was Patrick's fingers drumming nervously on an arm rest. Back home we took the four steps up to the first landing. On the right was Mom and Dad's bedroom, on the left, Glenn and Pat's room. It had one wall that Dad had covered in knotty pine, and two single beds with wagon wheel headboards. Their room was our meeting place, a safe place to be a child, a place to forget the terror of an unpredictable mother. As Glenn passed out crayons and sheets of paper, Pat reminded us of the rules of the Scribble game they invented.

"Okay, remember: I draw a scribble and pass it to the person to my right," Pat said, "and that person makes a picture out of it."

"Who wins?" Joan asked. She always wanted to win.

"Whoever draws the best picture," Pat replied patiently.

Daddy appeared in the doorway. He looked around at the group of us and smiled shamefacedly, the way he did when he felt powerless, when he had given in and become a child like us. "Your mother wants to talk to you," he said in a quiet voice.

Mom sat on the living room couch with five sharpened pencils and some ruled writing paper in front of her on the coffee table.

Her red platter hat was still on her head, and I saw Glenn's eyes go to the purse still on her wrist. Whenever Mom got sick, she liked to carry her purse around wherever she went. Her favorite was a red patent leather rectangular number with a gold clasp that she clicked open and close. "Children," she said in an oddly formal voice, "you were terrible in church today. I have never been so mortified in my life! Each of you will write one hundred times that you are sorry for the way you behaved. You are not to leave this room until you are done. Do you understand?" We all nodded. "One of you needs to help Margaret," she added dryly, and I tensed. She never called me Margaret unless her eyes were going to start that two-step.

Glenn handed each of us a piece of paper and a pencil and guided me to the dining room table.

"Can you help me write *I'm sorry I'm a pincherbug?*" I whispered. He printed the words neatly for me at the top of my paper. I stared at it in dismay. How was I ever to write anything so long one hundred times!

My mother sat in silence, looking straight ahead, an oppressive presence while we wrote. Glenn finished. So did Patrick and Sue. Even Joan got done. They each handed their papers to Mom and said they were sorry and escaped upstairs. I couldn't count past fifty and couldn't read what I was writing, so I didn't know if I was done. I picked up my paper and brought it to my mother. "Mommy, I'm sorry I pinched you. You wanna pinch me back?"

I was grateful for the glimmer of a smile from behind her mask. My mother was behind there somewhere.

* * *

"Mom, are we going to Grandma's house today?" Joan asked quietly at lunch a little while later. Since Joan was going through a phase where she didn't talk at the table, it was a surprise to hear her voice. Joan's light blue eyes and light blonde hair gave her a slightly ethereal appearance.

"Sure, honey," Mom said, to our relief.

"Do we have to listen to Uncle Jim's records?" Joan asked plaintively. Dad's older brother Jim still lived with their mom and dad. Joan didn't have a lot of patience for things she didn't like to do.

As we loaded into the car, Joan tripped on the curb and fell into the backseat laughing. There was an unexpected delight to Joan's laugh that made you float with her, that could change the way you felt about a whole day. Lilting and carefree, Joan's laugh infected us all. Maybe the day wouldn't be so bad after all.

Not wanting to be left behind, our black cocker spaniel Pogo pushed his way past Glenn at the front door and came bounding down the steps, ears flying. Pogo had started off being the O'Malleys' dog. One day he crossed the street and didn't want to go back again. Now he was ours. He jumped into his seat near the side window of the station wagon. Sue leaned over and rolled the window down for him so he could poke his head out. He liked to fly his long ears.

Mom still wore her church clothes. Daddy, who had changed into more comfortable clothes like the rest of us, paused and looked at Mom before turning on the ignition. He scrunched his face as he turned toward Mom. "Aren't you gonna change, Barb?"

"No, I'm fine," she said flatly, picking a string from her sweater. But I hadn't seen a string.

"All righty," Daddy said, shaking his head as he turned the ignition. His life was full of strangeness. It's only now that I realize how anxious he must have felt.

My father's parents lived in a house built just after the 1906 San Francisco earthquake and fire, when Oakland was booming. Grandma loved to laugh, but when she did, no noise came out—she'd exhale loudly and pound the table as her face turned red. And she was always up for a game of poker: if she didn't have enough change, we'd play for Cheerios. She kept a flask of brandy under her bed ("for my weak heart") and slept sitting up. She left her parents and ten siblings in Ireland to come to America alone when she was fifteen. Two years later she met James Kennedy, who was three years her senior and already working at a bank. They had four children over nine years and were very religious. Their social lives revolved around church functions, their four children (Daddy was the youngest), and home. She'd made sure that she and Grandpa had a house large enough to accommodate the family she created and cherished.

Grandpa was reserved. While Grandma laughed and pounded the table, he'd smile with only one side of his mouth curling up. Grandma greeted us at the door with a hug and a kiss and a "Ah, my little angels, I'm so glad you're all here." Her name was Johanna. Feeling safe in her arms, I held on to her longer than other Sundays. Her kind, round face came down to plant a kiss on my cheek. Her glasses were so thick that they distorted the shapes of her eyes, but as she pulled away, I thought I caught a twinkle. Each of Grandma's dresses was flowered and short-sleeved, with pockets filled with tissue. Her knee-high stockings only went halfway up her calves. Her shoes were thick-soled with open toes, specially made for her bunions. They were so heavy she pounded the floor when she walked. The many pot roasts, corned beefs, and pork loin suppers she'd fixed over the years seemed to cling to every wall in the house. I couldn't tell which of the three she was cooking that day.

Grandma turned her head a little to the side so she could see us through her thick glasses. "You kids wanna play a little poker?" she asked in her soft brogue with what vaguely looked like a wink. Dad, Uncle Jim, and Grandpa were soon belting away at their version of the Irish drinking song 'Harrigan': "K-E-double N-E-D-Y spells Kennedy, Kennedy…proud of all the Irish blood within me…devil a man to say a word agin' me … K-E-double N-E-D-Y you'll see … it's a name—that with shame—never has been connected with, Kennedy, that's me!" Having heard the song every Sunday as long as we could remember, we kids all started singing.

A mantle clock sat atop the TV. "To James P. Kennedy, 40 Years of Distinguished Service" it read in shiny gold letters. Grandpa had been the vault manager at the local branch of Bank of America. Wedding pictures of Dad and Mom, Auntie Sissy and Uncle Herb and Auntie Betty and Uncle Russ sat inside a glass case beside Dad's high school baseball trophy. Pictures of Christ and crucifixes held places of honor on the walls in this little room, as they did throughout the house.

At suppertime, I fell in line behind Joan, nodding eagerly to Grandma when she asked if I wanted some mashed potatoes. Smothered in mayonnaise and butter, they were easily my favorite food. "For you, darlin', a little bit more." Grandma put a big dollop of the potatoes on my plate before handing it to me. *Grandma loves me the most.* Unbeknownst to me, Grandma said the same thing to everyone.

Mom still wore her hat. It hovered like a flying saucer at Grandma's table, unsettling everybody. With her eyes blinking too fast, Mom looked like she belonged inside it. Maybe, if I sat next to her, she'd remember how not to be an alien. I squeezed into her chair and to my relief she scooted over to make room for me. As she passed behind Mom, Grandma's lips went limp. "Barb, can I take your hat?" She touched my mother's shoulder, but Mom shook her head without looking up.

Grandpa, a small, sturdy man with white hair receded to the perimeter of his head, sat at the end of the table, next to the laundry room where he often sneaked off to take a few puffs from his pipe.

Uncle Jim sat across from us. He was older than my father but had more hair, which he slicked back off his high forehead. His skin was soft and unlined like a baby's bottom. He suffered from epileptic seizures, which seemed to throw off his timing because he raised his eyebrows and smiled at odd moments. So far that day, we'd been lucky: he hadn't asked us to listen to his old 45s that skipped and sounded far away.

"Hey, Sus," he said at last, using his name for Sue, "You guys wanna come listen to my new 45s? I think you'll like 'em—they're pretty snappy," he clicked his fingers and held his hand next to his ear as he grinned.

Dad rolled his eyes so Sue would know that he, too, thought his brother was silly.

If she had been talking to one of us kids, Sue would have come back with a funny, sarcastic comment. Instead, she said sweetly, "Maybe later, Uncle Jim."

We'd finished dinner and were all playing poker when Mom said solemnly, "Jack, the kids have school tomorrow. We should go."

"But it's only 5:30. We haven't even had dessert," Dad protested.

She fixed him with that stern stare she'd worn earlier.

On our way out, Grandpa pinched each of our cheeks hard in farewell.

* * *

Joan lay on her bed tossing a small ball in the air and catching it again. "Mom was sure weird today," she said to the ceiling. The room the three of us girls shared was up more steps from the bedrooms below and had a ceiling that slanted up in the middle. Sue's bed was on the right, then counterclockwise, Joan's bed, then mine. The bedspreads were all chenille: Sue's blue, Joan's yellow, and mine—pink like Mom's. Our wooden headboards had a bookcase. Mine held my favorite toy, Mr. Pretzel (black-and-white nondescript face—round head, with long, skinny striped legs).

Sue lay on her stomach on her own bed. She was writing in her diary. "I know," she replied. She cocked her ear at the angry murmurs coming from our parents' bedroom.

"She didn't take her hat off all day," Joan persisted.

Sue heaved a sigh and rolled onto her side. She propped herself up on her elbow so that she could look straight at Joan. "I don't think she knew she had it on."

Joan sighed heavily, and then sighed again, a sign that she was troubled.

I tried to find a spot under the covers where my feet wouldn't be crushed by the pile of clothes on the end of my bed, but couldn't. I laid my glasses on the shelf of my headboard and fell asleep. In my dream, two men walked with my mother by a lake. I watched from a distance. They walked onto a dock and helped her into a rowboat, and then got in themselves. They rowed the boat out to the deep water and then jumped out. The boat began to sink. Mom sat calmly in her place, sinking with it. I ran onto the dock, with old pilings thundering under my feet. "Swim, Mommy," I yelled, but she didn't respond. "Swim, Mommy!" I screamed again. As she sank, I saw that her hands were tied to the boat.

Next day Dad hovered around the kitchen in his white shirt and black fireman's uniform and shiny badge. He still had most of his hair then, but it was thinning and turning gray. He touched Mom's shoulder. "Are you sure you don't want me to drop the kids off at school? I've got that fire prevention presentation over at the high school, but I could drop them off on the way."

"Jack, I'm fine, *really*," Mom said. She was knifing jelly onto a row of peanut butter sandwiches. She gave him a kiss on the cheek and left to go to the bathroom. We kids milled around, eating cereal, looking for shoes. While she was gone, Dad brought Mom's plastic medicine bottle into the eating area where we sat, dumped the pills into his hand, and counted them.

"Did she take it?" Glenn whispered. His white shirt ballooned on his skinny frame.

"Looks like it. There's one less pill than last night," Dad replied, relief in his voice.

From the time she had been institutionalized a couple of years before, my mother had taken two Thorazine pills a day. Dad managed to put the bottle back just as my mother returned to the kitchen.

"All righty, then, I guess I'll go," he said in a falsely hearty tone. He tried for a cheerful smile, but there was worry in his blue eyes. He hugged Mom. "You get some rest now."

Mom patted Dad's arm. "I will," she said. He glanced at his watch and picked up his black fireman's hat. The door shut behind him.

Mom's expression went blank. She threw the knife in the sink and closed her eyes the way she did when she was mad. But instead of yelling, she said playfully, "Hey, kids, it's early. Wanna watch a little TV?"

This was a rare treat. Sue and Joan rushed from their places at the kitchen table into the living room before Mom could change her mind. Patrick, ten, and Glenn, twelve, exchanged glances, then shrugged and followed them. I didn't feel like watching TV. Instead, I knelt before my cupboard to build another city out of cans. I had claimed a corner kitchen cabinet for my own. The shelves were filled with cans. I rearranged them, stacking them according to color and size. There was Star-Kist tuna, Jolly Green Giant creamed corn, green beans and peas, Hunt's tomato sauce, large cans of S&W cling peaches and half pears, and the hated cans of lima beans.

Usually when I played, I heard my mother's feet moving around the kitchen floor. That morning, they stayed in that one place. There was a smell just like when she was going to cook something, but it didn't smell as nice. I didn't like the smell.

I decided to make all tall buildings. As I moved the cans on the shelf, I noticed a small white box in the corner. Inside it were one, two, three, four, five, six, seven blue pills like the ones Daddy had been counting earlier. I closed the box and put it back. I would have to tell Glenn, because when Dad wasn't around, Glenn was the next best thing.

Without warning, my mother grabbed me by my elbow and pulled me into the living room. A can of creamed corn rolled across the linoleum floor. Sue sat on the couch, a rose, pink and green flowered couch with maroon fringe, but got up when Mom dragged me in. "Mom, shouldn't we be leaving for school now? We might be late," she said. Sue had green eyes, brown hair, and olive skin. In photos, she was the spitting image of Mom as a kid. The boys and Joan milled around uncertainly.

"No, I want to play a game!" Mom said with an exaggerated smile that reminded me of Miss Nancy on Romper Room. She clapped her hands. "All you kids go get on the couch for a minute." She opened her arms and herded us toward it.

Glenn balked. "A *game*? Mom, we're gonna be late."

"Oh, honey, this won't take long."

When we were sitting in a row on the overstuffed sofa, she announced that instead of going to school, we were going to Neverland. "It'll be fun. Remember—the pirates and Indians? I made arrangements for my friends, the Indians, to meet us there."

At first, I was excited—Mom had read us the Peter Pan story, and I wanted to go where my dreams could come true. I'd shouted, "I'll bet I can fly!" But Joan nudged me hard in the back and hissed in my ear, "Shut up, Peg!"

"What about Daddy?" I asked. Expecting another thump in the back from Joan, I tightened my shoulders and put my hand on the bridge of my nose to keep my glasses on, but no thump came. Daddy would be worried if he came home and we weren't there. We should at least leave a note for him that read, "Flying to Neverland."

But Mom didn't answer about Daddy.

"Say, kids, what time is it?" Buffalo Bob Smith rooted from the corner of our living room as the doorbell rang. "It's Howdy Doody time. It's Howdy Doody time. Bob Smith and Howdy

Doo say Howdy Doo to you. Let's give a rousing cheer 'cause Howdy Doody's here!"

The doorbell sounded again louder and was followed by knocking. Pogo started barking. I launched myself from the couch. When you're the youngest of five, being first is an accomplishment, even if it's to the door. But Patrick threw out his arm to stop me. Sue stared at the window. "Stop gawking!" Mom yelled. She grabbed Sue's arm and shook her until Sue's brown hair and pleated blue jumper swung back and forth, and then pushed her back down hard at the end of the couch next to Joan.

Sue dabbed at her sweater. Mom had scratched her and blood was seeping through. Patrick, his hair worn like Glenn's in a short wedge, gaped at Sue's wound. He had hazel eyes that looked green sometimes, and olive skin like Mom's. He had a round face and was slightly pudgy—we used to lie down on the kitchen floor and push out our stomachs in a competition to see whose was bigger—he usually won but only because he knew how to push harder. His white shirt touched my jumper, and I got a whiff of hair goop and toothpaste. His green eyes were watery. Sue pursed her lips together as she blinked back tears.

A *knock knock knock knock*. Through the shade, I could dimly make out our neighbor, Lou. I could hardly see her, but I knew she'd be wearing pink curlers in her hair and fuzzy slippers. Lou came to smoke cigarettes and drink coffee with Mom after we'd gone to school. But we hadn't left for school yet.

Glenn sat on Pat's left. He said, "Mom—did you turn off the oven? It smells like gas." I smelled it too. It smelled the way it did when mom turned on the big white knob on the oven to put in baked potatoes.

"Yes, Glenn, I turned it off."

Mom drew the curtains on Lou, and the room became dark, the way it was when we kids made a tent out of a blanket and sat underneath to tell stories. *Knock, knock!* "I will not have coffee with that woman today!" she told us. My eyes began to water. It hurt when I breathed in.

"Mom, we're gonna be late!" Glenn pleaded.

"Glenn." Mom's voice was sticky as honey. "Let's wait a minute and see if Peter Pan comes."

Peter Pan was fun, but I was in first grade now, and if I was late Sister Augustine Mary would close her eyes and shake her head at me slowly in disappointment.

Glenn hit his lap in frustration. At twelve, he was too old for Peter Pan. He shouted, "Mother! This is ridiculous!" His Adam's apple jumped in this throat.

The pounding moved to the back of the house.

Mom's eyes darted as she paced back and forth in front of us. She wasn't her usual self. Her green eyes were shiny. Her mouth was dead. I wanted to change her back into my real mommy, the one who called me *Egetha* and let me cuddle with her in the chair, where I inhaled her mixture of face foundation and cigarettes as her knitting needles crossed over to exchange loops as she wrapped her arms around me and continued knitting. My father would be on the couch reading the newspaper, occasionally looking up to watch the news. The small green-screened television sat within a blonde wood cabinet with gold mesh-covered speakers. When a friend of mine bragged that his family had a color TV, I told him we did too—a green and gold one.

I wished I could borrow the Viewmaster my friend had gotten from a place called Disneyland. It changed pictures when you clicked it. I'd click us to the slide of the knitting mother instead of being stuck in the view with this pacing wild-eyed mother across the oval green rug. Joan yanked at her blonde hair. It was normally straight, but like me and Sue, she had the tortured curl of a Toni Home Permanent. Watching her twirl it made me dizzy. The smell was stronger. Our couch seemed to rock like a raft stuck in choppy water. I tucked my feet under me so the alligators couldn't bite them off and leaned against Joan's shoulder, not much higher than mine.

I focused on the baby finger of Joan's right hand. The nail still had some pink nail polish she had neglected to remove. She'd removed all the polish from my nails the night before, even though I'd begged her to leave it on. "The nuns will whack your hands, Peg, if you wear polish to school," she'd said, wiping it away. I fought to open my lips so I could warn her about the polish on her baby fingernail, but my lips stubbornly refused. My eyes fell shut.

Bang, bang, *BANG!* The door into the dining room shook like a jackhammer. And then it burst open, and we all turned. Lou stood in the doorway with a kitchen towel over her nose.

"Holy Mother of God!" she cried.

Lou's wiry red hair, normally combed into a bob, stood up in clumps like the half corncobs Mom served us at dinner, and she still wore her bathrobe and slippers. She rushed around the room opening the windows. I watched her, perplexed. She had obviously gone nuts.

Lou ran to Mom and hugged her tight. "Thank God you're okay, Barbara! I thought we'd lost you all."

Mom stood stiff. Lou took a step back. "Barbara," she said breathlessly, "I saw the station wagon out front. I told myself you should have left with the kids by now. I rang the bell and knocked, no one answered. I ran to the back door ... Barbara—you have to be more careful. For God's sake, you've got to remember to turn off the oven and close the oven door!"

Mom crossed her arms. Standing next to Lou in Capri pants and shell, she looked like Mom again, her auburn hair neatly pinned and sprayed—until you saw her eyes. Lou's hands shot up to her mouth. *"No, No, Barb! These are your children!"* Awareness dawned on the older kids. Glenn shook his hands in front of him; Sue and Joan whimpered. Patrick's arm wrapped round my shoulders. His body shook. Mom leaned in toward Lou and said, "My people, the Indians, finally came to take us to Neverland, where we belong. I wasn't going to be left behind."

There was silence then. But if either woman had lit a cigarette at that moment, we could all have been transported to Neverland in no time flat.

Glenn's hands went to his forehead, and he bent over his knees. After what seemed like a long time, he raised his head. "Okay, you guys," he said tiredly. He stood up. "Patrick, take them outside. I'll call Daddy. Then I'll call school and let them know we're gonna be late."

Mom leaned against the wall in the dining room. "Here we go." She rolled her eyes. Lou stayed near her, still in shock, her mouth open in dismay.

We filed outside to sit quietly on the lawn. Dad drove up in his maroon car with Oakland Fire Department stamped on the door just as Father Hecht arrived in his black parish sedan. They walked toward us together, Father Hecht's black cassock catching between his fat legs. Dad smiled tightly at our small anxious faces. Sweat covered his brow and upper lip. He would make everything all right. The priest's lips softened in sympathy. We stayed on the lawn as Dad and the priest walked up the porch stairs. At the top, Father Hecht touched Dad's arm. "I'll take the children to school, Jack."

Dad sucked in his upper lip. He was pale. "I guess that would be the best thing for them, Father?"

"I wouldn't recommend changing the children's schedule today. I'll let the Sisters know that they've had a difficult morning."

We children crept in behind Daddy and Father Hecht and sat on the braided throw rug on the floor. Lou squeezed Dad's hand. She squinted her teary eyes. "Call me if you need me, Jack." Glenn removed the top of the hat box kept behind Mom's rose-colored chair. Inside were the clay people and wardrobe and furniture that he and Pat had fashioned over the past few months. Glenn distributed lumps of different-colored clay. We began kneading our blobs of purple, green, and orange. I saw Daddy rubbing his forehead as he stood next to the priest. The priest spoke quietly to Mom. But standing by the open window, her eyes vacant, Mom seemed to have already flown away. Off in the distance a siren whirred getting louder as it came closer until the sound outside made me cover my ears. When she turned, my mother looked terrified. Dad tried to put his arm around her, but she threw it off. Father Hecht's face was flushed. He approached our little circle slowly as though afraid that we might rise like a flock of startled birds and fly against the walls and windows. A warm breeze blew through the open windows.

Two men in white clothes carried a gurney in the open front door. The globs of clay sat forgotten in our hands as we watched them approach Mom.

"Come, children, it's time to go to school," Father Hecht said urgently, as he tore his own eyes from the paramedics. Obediently, we all stood and moved toward the front door. Lou came up beside us, hoping to shield our eyes with her body, but we could see the men take hold of Mom.

"My babies! My babies! Jack, how could you?" My mother screamed as she twisted and tried to escape. *"I'm not leaving this house!"* Father Hecht hurried us to the door. *"I'M NOT LEAVING!"* Mom shrieked again. But she was on the gurney now, and the straps were around her arms and legs, locking her down.

The men carried Mom through the front door as we started to pull away from the curb in Father Hecht's car. Daddy stood at the front door, head facing skyward, his body quivering like a flame.

Chapter 2

❦

Jolly Green Giant

Daddy tried at first to keep us at home and take care of us himself. He often had to leave for work late, and then take off early. Dad's station captain, who had kids of his own, looked the other way.

Having a mom at Napa State Hospital wasn't like when my classmate Marie's mother had gotten sick in kindergarten, and we all had made pretty cards for her. No one ever asked us how our mother was, or ever offered to say a prayer for her to get better. Mental illness scared people. If you had it, you didn't admit it. If your mother had it, you prayed that no one would find out. But everybody knew about my mother. I heard whispering at school, and sometime kids would stop talking when I walked up to them. The stress soon gave my father migraine headaches. Many days, he came home early, and I could tell that from the way he moved and held his head. He was in pain. We kids learned to close the drapes and walk in our socks, voices low.

He tried farming us out to Mom's parents—we called them "Nana" and "Dad" (which explains why we called our father "Daddy") who owned a white clapboard sided duplex on Voltaire Avenue in Oakland maybe a mile from the Oakland Zoo. Mom's dad, now retired, had been in the lumber business and was a good carpenter—for a hobby he built big wooden desks with lots of cubbies and a pull-down writing table. He liked to wear fedora-style hats and had a thick belly. He always had a stash of black licorice button candy in a white bag by his chair. He'd pat his chair for you to come and sit with him. I was always flattered when he asked me, and don't remember him doing anything that made me feel uncomfortable, but both Sue and my cousin Mary (Mary is one year older than Sue) said he fondled them, but Sue didn't tell Daddy then. Once, my Mom's father took my cousin Mary in his car and stuck his tongue in her mouth. Luckily, she told her father, and he yelled at my grandfather and threatened that he wouldn't allow him to see the kids anymore if he tried anything again. I believe that there's a chance that he abused my Mom, and that's why he favored her when she was young and why her mother never seemed to care for her. Maybe it helped to drive Mom mad, I don't know.

Nana was about five feet tall. She wasn't warm and cuddly like my other grandma and complained a lot about her aches and pains. She had her first psychotic episode and was hospitalized when she was in her early forties. She had shelves filled with a collection of glass animals that we weren't allowed to touch, funny little blown glass creatures with stripes and long trunks. When Joan and I accidentally knocked a few of the glass animals off the shelf while playing jacks, Nana had a cold, cold hissy fit.

Luckily, Dad's sister Colette, whom we called Auntie Sissy, offered to help just as she had the last time Mom was hospitalized. She adored Daddy, her younger brother by three years. She would take us during the week, and Dad would bring us home on weekends. Auntie Sissy was five feet, three inches tall; she was slender, with short black curls tucked behind her ears. She wore short-sleeved collared shirts under sweaters with the sleeves up above her elbows and Capri pants and flats (like Audrey Hepburn in *Funny Face*) and had a mischievous grin.

Auntie Sissy had four children of her own: Skip was sixteen, Bobby, twelve, Jamie, ten, and Mike, six. Uncle Herb was a successful electrician with his own company. The Bowen family lived in the Oakland hills in a tasteful home overlooking the bay. They had a chic wraparound white couch, color television, sophisticated stereo system, a piano they let us pound on whenever we wanted, and a freezer always stocked with Neapolitan ice cream ("A flavor for everyone," Auntie Sissy would say).

Uncle Herb had a cleft chin and a booming voice designed to strike terror into the hearts of large, misbehaving children. The impact on smaller children was even greater. When Daddy dropped us off that first Sunday night, he answered the door. The five of us stood on the porch behind our father, each with suitcase and pillow, with our uniforms hanging from our fingers on hangers.

"Well, there they are! Colette, come see what the cat dragged in!" he yelled into the kitchen, and we all giggled.

Auntie Sissy and Dad hugged each other tight. When Dad tried to thank my aunt and uncle, tears welled up in his eyes. Uncle Herb patted his arm. "Jack, we're happy to do it." We kissed Daddy good-bye and crowded gladly into the Bowen house.

At dinner, all nine of us kids ate at the kitchen table, while Auntie Sissy and Uncle Herb ate in their formal dining room.

"I'll bet I can stick peas to the ceiling," Bobby said in a loud whisper one night at dinner. He smiled wide, revealing the space between his front teeth. Bobby thrived on danger. He was twelve, like Glenn.

Glenn narrowed his eyes at Bobby. "I'll bet you can't."

Bobby turned his spoon around, balanced the pea and then let it loose. The pea fell back to the floor.

We all screeched in delight, so he tried again. This time it stuck for a second, then it fell. He continued to try until flattened peas

31

lay all over the linoleum floor. That's when Uncle Herb walked in. "What the hell are you doing in here?" he boomed, his gaze automatically settling on Bobby.

"Trying to stick peas to the ceiling?" Bobby answered meekly. He raised his shoulders as if to deflect a blow.

Uncle Herb moved his face menacingly close to Bobby's. "You do that one more time and I'll knock your block off—you understand?" My fingers dug into my legs.

"Yes, sir," Bobby answered timidly. Uncle Herb left the room. Our gaze swung to Bobby, expecting to see remorse.

Instead, he whispered gleefully, "Okay, one last time," and punched the end of the spoon to send the pea soaring. The pea stuck. Forgetting ourselves, we all cheered. Bobby knew the cheer would bring Uncle Herb and ran out of the room laughing hysterically.

Uncle Herb charged into the kitchen just in time for the slackened pea to land right on his cheek, from where it miraculously managed to roll down his face to the cleft of his chin. We all sucked in our breath. He twisted his mouth in disgust and wiped the green mash off his face. "That goddamned kid," he said. Then, to our surprise, he started to laugh. The laugh was deep and jovial like that of the Jolly Green Giant. He shook his head, wiped his finger, and went back into the dining room. It felt good to see someone yell and then go back to being normal.

It could be done. Perhaps Mom could learn to do it.

Chapter 3

❧❧

Dishes in my Cupboard

Pat, Sue, and I all had birthdays in late September and early October. With my mother still in the hospital, Daddy was determined to do his best to make them special. For his birthday dinner, Pat asked for apple fritters, deep-fried dough filled with apple pie filling. He was remembering Mom's delicious apple fritters.

Patrick got the first made-by-Dad apple fritter. He smiled as he chewed. "These are the best I've ever had, Dad." Daddy looked pleased. Patrick brought his napkin up to his mouth and seemed to hold it there for a long time.

Glenn and Sue got theirs next. Sue took a bite and soon she, too, covered her mouth with her napkin. Glenn winced as he munched. Patrick wiped his mouth again with his napkin until his plate was empty. His lips were pressed together hard to keep from laughing. I was anxious to taste what was so funny. My first bite tasted like oily pancake. I searched in vain for any semblance of apple. Joan tried to give hers to Pogo, but he sniffed the greasy morsel and walked away.

We all watched Dad take his first bite. "Ugh! These are awful!" He exclaimed. He spat the bite back onto his plate. "I can't believe you guys are eating them. I guess I forgot to put in the apple filling." Patrick produced a napkin full of fritter from under the table, and we all laughed until our sides hurt.

I thought Sue would be excited to turn ten, but she woke up on her birthday with a sour expression, threw on her clothes, and told Joan and me she was going to ride Glenn's bike with a friend.

I heard her hit the rusted latch that held together the slightly lopsided doors of our garage, and the wheel on Glenn's old bike scrape against the bent fender as she coasted the bike down the driveway to the street.

At dinner that night, Dad stood at the stove in Mom's apron, frying bacon and scrambling eggs for the birthday dinner Sue had requested. He turned the eggs with the rubber spatula. "Where's Sue?" he asked everybody. "She should be home by now."

We were at the table when Sue finally came home, her face rosy from the outdoors but with the same sullen expression on her face. When my father asked her where she'd been, she shrugged her shoulders. "Cathy and I were just riding around and stuff."

She went up to her room, and we heard a shriek. We all rushed up, even Dad. There, on the other side of Sue's bed, was a brand-new bike. Dad grinned. Sue's grin split across her face and seemed likely to stay there forever.

We got to talk with Mom on Saturday mornings while she was in the hospital. We got one call for all three of our birthdays since they all fell within the same week. We each got to talk with her for just a few seconds since she was calling from a pay phone outside their eating hall. The fact that she joked (she said Patrick, who'd turned eleven, was "turning into an old man") and her words didn't jumble together was comforting.

* * *

Finally, it was my birthday, with beef burgers, fries, and shakes from Jerry's, where the cool high school kids hung out and flirted. When at last Daddy brought me my present, I ripped open the paper. Through the clear plastic cover was a set of blue and white dishes with matching cups and saucers, plates and bowls, cream and sugar holders and teapot.

I threw the paper on the floor and buried my face in the couch. I didn't want dishes. If I put them in my cupboard, they'd mess up my city of cans. Dishes were for mommies, and Mommy was gone.

Through the couch pillow, I heard, "Peg, I'm sorry. I thought you'd like them." Dad stroked my hair. "Maybe we can go get you a different present later." When I didn't respond, I heard his footsteps going away.

I sat up to see a ring of mad faces. Joan snapped her tongue behind her front teeth with disdain. "You could have *pretended* you liked it, Peg," she hissed. Her freckles stood out on her red face.

"You need to tell Daddy you're sorry, Peg," Sue joined in.

Glenn nodded. Patrick heaved a sigh, as if to say there was no getting out of doing what I had to do. I rammed my face back in the couch cushion. Four sets of feet ran up the stairs, and a bedroom door slammed.

I picked up the dish set and forced myself to walk into the kitchen. Dad sat at the table reading the *Oakland Tribune*. When my father was upset or hurt, or even excited, the newspaper provided cover for him to keep his cool. He looked up.

"Well, *there* she is." he said it as if I'd been lost and he had suddenly found me. It was his signal that all was forgiven.

I set the box down on the table and stepped back. If I were closer, he would hug me, but I didn't deserve a hug.

"I miss Mommy," I said. I wiped the tears that started to flow behind my glasses with the backs of my hands.

"I miss her too, honey. I'm sure she misses you a lot." Dad reached over and fluffed my hair.

The thought of Mom missing me made me feel better. I sniffed and wiped my nose on my arm for lack of a tissue.

I carried the box to my cupboard. Since Mom was gone, my supply of cans had dwindled. I moved the cans to the bottom shelf, rebuilding my city of cans there.

I pulled the top off the box. The dishes had houses, flowers, and trees and creatures wrapped around the edges that looked like the dragon in the Chinese story Sister had read us at school. They were pretty!

Within minutes, the box was empty, and my shelf gleamed with cups, plates, bowls, cream and sugar containers, a serving spoon and fork, and a gravy boat. I sighed happily.

I had my own dishes, just like Mommy. But I had my city of cans, too.

Chapter 4

❧❧

Swimming Again

Two weeks later, the doctor called to say it was okay for us to visit Mom. Daddy packed a picnic lunch; and since there was so much lawn up at Napa State Hospital, he packed our croquet set as well. The drive took over one hot hour. To pass the time, Joan and I played patty cake. We were excited about seeing Mom, and that made our pats harder than normal. By the time we reached the hospital, my palms burned. Once we'd parked, Daddy told us to find a spot for a picnic and set off across the green expanse toward the white columned building in the distance. They didn't allow children inside the hospital.

Glenn and Pat found a shady spot on a knoll beneath a big tree and laid out the blanket. Glenn pulled out a pack of cards and asked Sue to play. Pat settled in with his drawing pad and pencil. Joan unpacked the tuna sandwiches, apples, Cracker Jack boxes, and Cokes. Although I'd promised Joan that I'd help, I spent most of my time staring at the hospital entrance.

"Peg, they'll be here in a minute ... geez," Joan said.

A door on the side of the building opened, and Mom and Dad came out hand in hand. I ran toward Mom so fast that I almost knocked her down when I reached her. I burrowed my head into her stomach. When Mom wasn't doing a series of shock treatments, she worked at the beauty parlor on the grounds of the Napa State Hospital giving perms, so she smelled of perm solution. Though her smell brought tears to my eyes and her arms around me weren't as strong as before, she was my mom, and she was back. She wore a sleeveless seersucker dress that I remembered from an outing to get ice cream a few months before. That time, she'd worn red high heels, and the dress had flattered her. This time, she wore white laced shoes and her dress was wrinkled and baggy.

"When are you coming home, Mommy?" I searched her face to make sure it was her.

"Pretty soon, honey, pretty soon," she said. She stroked my hair as we walked toward my brothers and sisters on the knoll.

My siblings stood and hugged her when she got there. "Oh my gosh, Glenn, you've gotten tall, honey," she said. She held him away from her so she could look at him. Glenn stood up straighter. We had changed while she was gone. The family had gone on without her.

She turned to Sue. "Susu, I like your hair in a flip like that," she said, touching where my sister's hair flipped up. Blushing with pleasure, Sue looked over her raised shoulder like a screen goddess and batted her eyes. Glenn made a face, and Pat pretended to stick his finger down his throat.

"Joanie Bologne—I see you've laid out a nice picnic lunch for us here," Mom said.

"I helped too, Mommy," I said. Joan rolled her eyes.

"At-arick," Mom said, using her nickname for Pat as she knelt next to him on the blanket.

Pat handed her his drawing and wrapped his bottom incisor around his upper incisor in anticipation. "I drew this for you."

Though he was only eleven, the sketch he had drawn looked as though Mom held a mirror in her hand. The drawing was an exact replica of her.

"That's great, Pat," Dad said. He sat down next to Mom. He always seemed surprised by Pat's artistic talent because, as he often said, he himself could barely draw stick figures.

"Patrick, you have a gift." Mom kissed him on the forehead.

We had all crowded around our mother. "Hey, Mom, we brought our croquet set," Joan said. She kneaded Mom's fingers like clay as she held her hand.

"Jack, are you sure it's all right?" Mom asked nervously.

"Oh, I think it's fine, Barb." Daddy threw his car keys to Glenn. "Go get the croquet set out of the trunk, sport."

Glenn and Pat found a level area nearby. "Are you guys playing?" Glenn yelled up to Mom and Dad as we gathered around the first two wickets with our mallets.

"No, honey, you go ahead. We'll just watch," Mom said with a smile.

I didn't mind. Nobody did. Just being near her was enough. She didn't need to play.

The sun filtered through the trees to make shadow patterns on the croquet course. As I struggled to hit my ball through the first hoop, I noticed Glenn looking off between some trees. I followed his eyes. A strange parade of people with slumped shoulders and messy hair followed a man in a white coat. Glenn told me not to stare, but I couldn't help it. One of them waved at us as if he knew us. I waved back.

A patient with short dark hair stood in front of the group of trees. Instead of going for his ball, Glenn walked over to him. The person covered his mouth as if he was laughing. Was he a man or a boy? When Glenn approached him, the fellow looked down at the ground and scratched the top of his head, his arm white and sickly in the sun. He was the same size as Glenn. The stranger nodded eagerly at whatever it was Glenn said, and my brother brought him over to the game. "Who's that?" I asked as

39

they came near to where I stood halfway between the second and third wickets. I could see he was a grown man. Glenn turned to him. "What's your name?" he asked politely.

The man had heavy dark eyebrows and bright blue eyes. "Anthony." His teeth were black. His mother must not have reminded him to brush!

Glenn handed him a blue ball and a blue striped mallet. "Here you go, Anthony. You can be blue." He pointed him toward the first wicket. I was thrilled—I was no longer in last place!

To the right, I could hear bits and pieces of Mom and Dad's conversation. "I have to get out of here, Jack," Mom said. "Talk to the doctor, please."

I edged up the knoll in time to see Dad put his arm around Mom's shoulders. "I will, Barb." He must have wanted his wife home; but he must have also been scared of a relapse.

Anthony raised his mallet over his head like a hatchet. "Stop!" Dad screamed. He charged down the slight incline toward Anthony, stopping short when Anthony hit the ball. Anthony glanced fearfully at Daddy's shoes, dropped his mallet and hurried off.

"Daddy, you scared him," I reprimanded.

My father put his hands to his head and heaved a sigh. "Honey, you just never know."

* * *

Mom still wasn't home by Halloween. Since we wanted to trick-or-treat in our own neighborhood, Dad picked us up after school. Joan helped fit me with the ballerina outfit she'd worn the year before. It was a little snug.

"Peg, you have to stop eating so much," she said. I sucked in my stomach so she could zip up the tutu. "You're getting as big as a house." I was always hungry. Food seemed to fill a big hole inside me. When my siblings took one piece of bread, I'd take two. On the rare occasions that we had pie or cake, I'd try to sneak a second piece.

"Can a person really get as big as a house?" I asked.

"Yep, if they eat enough," Joan answered matter-of-factly. That didn't sound right. For the first time, I questioned my sister's wisdom, but I didn't say anything.

The Tuesday after Halloween, John F. Kennedy won the presidential election. The following weekend, Grandma gathered all of her children and their families at her house to celebrate the new Irish Catholic president. Highballs flowed. Uncle Jim set his phonograph up in the kitchen so everyone could dance. Daddy danced with Auntie Sissy and Grandma with Uncle Herb. Patrick swept around the floor with me balanced on his feet while Glenn spun Sue and Cousin Jamie. Joan grimaced as she be-bopped with Uncle Jim as Cousin Bobby banged a pot with a spoon out to the laundry room, where Grandpa sat smack dab in the middle in a lawn chair smoking his pipe. I ached for Mom, who loved to dance.

Grandma stood up and made a toast. "Here's to Jack Kennedy moving to the White House!" Everyone clinked their glasses and yelled, "Hear, hear!"

I was horrified. Was this what the celebration was about? Daddy was going to move us to a white house? How would Mommy find us when she got out of the hospital?

Patrick found me in the television room, my head buried in the back cushion. He sat down next to me on the leather chair and touched my shoulder. "What's wrong, Peggle?"

I raised my head and thumbed my glasses back into place. "I don't want to move to a white house!" I sobbed. "How will Mom find us?"

Pat looked at me quizzically then started to laugh. "That's not Daddy, Peg, that's our new president. His name is Jack Kennedy too."

The following Saturday, Dad got a call that Mom could come home.

She was swimming again.

Part II

Sit or Dance

1965-1979

Chapter 5

❦

Gray Walls

In 1961, the year after she lined us up on the couch and turned on the gas, Mom pulled us out of St. Louis Bertrand and enrolled us in Oakland public schools. Though she said it was because the nuns interfered when she kept Glenn home with asthma, I'm sure our move had more to do with getting away from people who knew what she tried to do. My parents sold the house with my special can cupboard and, with the money saved on parochial school tuition, bought a new house high on a hill above the Oakland Zoo.

Public school was a breeze. At night, Glenn, Pat, and Sue, who now went to Elmhurst Junior High School, taught Joan and me the latest Motown dance moves that they'd learned during their lunchtime dances—a brilliant innovation from a beleaguered school administration. Elmhurst Jr. High School was a 1930s beige stucco building with bars over the windows and a gravel field where Pat claimed he got cut up playing football. Most of the students were black—the rest were white and Latino. Glenn managed to become student body president (it helped that JFK was president at the time), and both Pat and Sue became presidents of their respective classes. Pat scoffed to Glenn, "The only real thing you have to do as student body president is to choose the music for the lunchtime dances." He also said the only reason he was elected class president was, "During my campaign, I convinced the biggest black guy on campus to wear a diaper and play John John." He talked other friends into playing Jackie and Caroline and introduced them in his campaign speech as his family.

I got my own room. No coins were tossed, no sticks were chosen; Joan and Sue simply said I could have it. I soon found, though, that a pretty room all your own can be lonely. Worse yet, when I knocked on my sisters' door all conversation ceased.

By the end of third grade in 1963, Mom was tired of the drive down the winding road to school, and she insisted on moving again. She and Dad sold the house and, for the first time, realized a good profit. We had sixty days to find a new house. Mom had heard that nearby San Leandro had better public schools than Oakland, so with money in their pockets to burn, every Sunday Mom and Dad crammed us into the car to cruise San Leandro for "Open House" signs. The City of Oakland required that firemen live within twenty minutes of their fire station, which was why we stayed in the area.

We found a winner: a house on a corner lot with wooden lodge-style beams in the living room and hardwood floors and a front yard perfect for croquet. There was money left over for new furniture. Trusting Glenn's eye for style, Mom let him loose in Kay's Furniture Store. Striding past the dowdy traditional displays, Glenn chose a contemporary white couch, a burnt-orange side chair, and an oversized chair in green and black tweed for the living room. For the den he chose maple loveseats with wagon-wheel sides.

The house even had a built-in dishwasher. Oddly, the original owners had chosen maroon tiles to border the yellow appliances—a jarring combination. Thank God they'd tied it all together with that pink dishwasher! Maroon and pink must have been hot colors when the house was built just after the war, as they'd used them in the two bathrooms, too. Pink also happened to be Mom's favorite color.

In my mind, new furniture and that pink dishwasher propelled us from lower-middle class to middle-middle class. Our gray Formica kitchen set had been replaced with a trendier faux wood table and boldly flowered gold and olive green chairs. Pink and red camellias surrounded the windows on both sides. Dad spent hours pruning the plants and edging the lawn. It was one of the few things over which he wielded some control. Though Mom and Dad had bought some new furniture, they didn't have the money to buy a dining room set. Our china, awaiting a hutch, was crammed into boxes in the dining room alongside a miniature pool table.

Though larger than our last house, this one had fewer bedrooms, so I once again shared a room with Sue and Joan. I was thrilled. No more missed conversations! Originally intended as a rec room, our bedroom took up the entire upstairs. Sue and Joan's beds were at opposite ends of one wall of the large rectangle, and mine was in the middle of the wall across from them.

"Who needs a headboard and box spring?" Sue asked the day we moved in. She plunked her mattress down on the floor in the corner. Other moms would have complained that they'd paid good money for that headboard and to put that box spring back, but not my mother. When she was normal, Mom was easygoing. I imagine she was too grateful for not being sick to agonize over little things like mattresses on the floor.

Joan and I switched to Roosevelt Elementary school in San Leandro, Glenn started at San Leandro High School, and Sue, at Bancroft Jr. High, but Pat wanted to finish out his year as president of Elmhurst Jr. High,'s ninth-grade class. Years later Pat told me he was walking down the hall one day with his friend, a black girl he'd chosen as his class vice president, when another girl came up and started arguing with her. Within minutes, the other girl had stabbed his friend in the head. Pat heard the sound of the knife going in. Pat's friend died. Mom immediately switched him to San Leandro High after that—an all-white high school with one black student, who, interestingly enough, was elected student-body president.

A few weeks after we moved in, when I asked Mom if she would drive me to school, she answered in that cold voice: "Only if you've ironed the blouse that goes with your uniform." Somehow, her entire memory of my second-grade year in which my big toe had been mashed by a wooden lunch bench and third grade when my glasses were crunched by a tetherball on the playground of E. Morris Cox public school on Ninety-eighth Ave. had vanished. I walked to school my arms huddled against the cold. I tried not to step on the cracks, but they seemed wider than ever.

That night Mom didn't appear for dinner. She stayed in bed, drawing the pink chenille spread up to her chin, drinking cup after cup of coffee from the electric pot she'd put on the nightstand next to her bed, having a lively conversation with herself.

When I came home from school the next day, the house was empty. Mom's nightgown lay on her closet floor, tossed there when she dressed hurriedly while the police waited in the living room. Her lipstick-smeared coffee cup and overflowing ashtray sat on the nightstand, like drunken guests left over from the night before. I threw myself on her bed and hugged her pillow, inhaling her fragrance of foundation makeup, Heaven Sent perfume, and smoke.

For the next couple of months, I couldn't bear to look at her empty chair at the kitchen table. She was at Agnews State Hospital in Santa Clara near San Jose (formerly the Agnews Insane Asylum where she was first institutionalized by her father).

When she came back, she was like a mail-order wife—determined to resume her role as the mother of the family. Having gotten used to washing and folding our own clothes and cooking our own meals during her absence, it was disconcerting to have her insisting on taking over those tasks again, as if she were a newly arrived servant. For the first couple of days, she was afraid to show too much emotion, as though that might indicate that she was still sick. She smiled but didn't laugh, and she spoke almost in a whisper. It was only on the third day that I knew she was really back when—after making her daily call to her mother who whined about every ache and pain—she turned to me and said, "Egetha, just shoot me if I ever get like that."

As I lay squished beside her on the maple loveseat in the den, my head resting in her lap as she gently stroked my hair, I spied something dark on the underside of her arm and looked closer: her entire arm was black and blue! I looked at her other arm. It was just as badly bruised.

"What happened, Mom?" I asked, as to a hurt child.

Her lips crumpled. For a second, I thought she'd deny that she'd ever been institutionalized. And yet, there were those bruises. "Shock treatments, honey. The doctor said they'd help me get better." She shifted her gaze to the window. The conversation was over. I didn't press for more.

Later that night, as Joan slept and Sue read on her mattress on the floor, I rose on my elbow. "Sue, what are shock treatments?" I knew Sue would give it to me straight. She made it her business to know the names of Mom's medications and their purpose.

Sue looked up. "They hook a mental patient up to a machine that makes them have seizures, kind of like Uncle Jim's epileptic seizures."

"Why are Mom's arms bruised?"

"They have to hold you down."

I learned later that she had electroshock treatment twice a week. Promptly at 7:30 a.m. treatment patients were herded, begging, pleading, crying, and resisting into the gymnasium and seated around the edge of the room. A long row of screens lay between them and the terrifying shock-treatment table on the other side of the screen. In order to save time, one or more patients were called behind the screen to sit down and take off their shoes while the patient who preceded them was still on the table convulsing and shaking after the electric shock had knocked them unconscious.

One attendant stood at the head of the table to put the rubber heel in the patient's mouth so he wouldn't chew his tongue during the convulsive stage. On either side of the table three other attendants held him down. After the electroshock, patients were given a heavy doze of Thorazine, which made them so foggy-headed and zombielike that they needed help with bathing and eating, and they had to be escorted around the hospital grounds.

* * *

June, 1966

It was almost the end of sixth grade. A poster of the Austrian cottage that Glenn bought for Joan at Cost Plus hung on the wall next to her bed, cheerful against the gloomy gray that the previous owners had painted the walls. My parents didn't paint walls. Painting walls meant that you were making the house your own, and doing that meant you were staying. Joan gnawed on the red licorice whip she'd bought at the Quik Stop we stopped at on the way home from school. Though the Heath bars and Butterfingers had shrieked "Buy Me!" I'd chosen a large dill pickle. The year before, in fifth grade, I'd vowed never to set foot in a Chubbette clothing section again. But as soon as I opened the pickle package, its juice spilled all over my lap. I smelled like a plump deli sandwich.

Although neither of my parents had been to college themselves, they expected all five of us to go. Mom had taken a job at an employment agency to help pay for Glenn's college expenses. Although Mom hadn't been employed since before she and Dad were married, I knew she'd be good at finding jobs for people. I could see her taking the hand of some poorly dressed, sad-eyed woman. "Don't you worry, honey," she'd say, "We'll find you a job in no time."

For a while, during the years of my middle childhood, life was normal. Mom stirred her Cream of Wheat on the yellow electric stove that matched the yellow oven. Though nicotine and coffee had stained her Easter Bunny teeth, we'd nicknamed Mom "Mother Rabbit." She'd get her teeth cleaned, she said, just as soon as she paid off all of our dental and orthodontic bills with money from her new job. Glenn and Pat had both worn braces to correct crooked front teeth. We girls were luckier: our teeth had come in straight.

Years of Thorazine and other antipsychotic drugs had taken their toll on my mother: a trade-off of premature physical degeneration for sanity. Her upper arms, once toned from hoisting five small children, had become flabby. Her auburn hair was brassy, the result of a recent heavy-handed application of henna rinse. She wore puffy bangs over her forehead and a tubular puff at the back of her head which, after teasing and pinning, was aggressively sprayed into place. Her knee-high white go-go boots (think *Shindig*) gapped around her thin calves, her short brown skirt was tight around her waist but had extra room in the derriere, and a sleeveless royal blue turtleneck sweater was heavily taxed by her ample chest. Her foundation makeup caked around the lines on her face and neck. Her lips were smacking red.

"Good morning," I said, putting a couple of pieces of bread in the toaster and sitting down next to Patrick, who wore a trace of a mustache above his upper lip and sideburns grown to the bottom of his ear. His hair, in defiance of school rules, hung well past his collar. His face had thinned, his hazel eyes had deepened in intensity, and his freckles had long since disappeared. I tried not to notice how handsome he'd become.

Joan sauntered in wearing a neatly fitted blouse and skirt and brown suede knee-high boots. She knew how to make the most of our annual back-to-school shopping treks to Montgomery Ward's basement, having an eye for fashion even when there was little to choose from. Her straight blonde hair hung just above her shoulders with bangs making an arc below her eyebrows. Her blue eyes were wide awake from the moment they opened, no matter how early.

Sue made her entrance in a long purple cloak and thick black shoes that she'd found at St. Vincent de Paul's. She reached for a banana out of the fruit bowl that Mom always kept on the table, slipping it into her pocket like a detective sliding a gun into her trench coat. Sue rode up the street on her bike and disappeared around the corner. Once out of sight, I knew, she would light a cigarette.

Dad came in the front door just as we were leaving for school. As with Mom, the last six years had taken their toll on him. His hair, now mostly gray, had receded to the sides of his head save some wisps of hair on top. He had been working three days on, four off at the firehouse. He and Mom kissed and slapped each other's bottoms as they went through the door in opposite directions.

"Short but sweet," Dad said, blue eyes crinkling as he smiled and watched Mom walk down the front steps in her high-heeled boots.

"That's me, Daddy," Mom said in a little girl's voice, "The baby is short but *very* sweet!" She blew him a kiss.

Later that afternoon, I tapped on Glenn's door even though it was ajar. In our large family, privacy was a big issue. He waved me in with a smile. Books crowded the three shelves that ran the length of the wall next to the door. A poster of Brigitte Bardot in a bikini, Rodin's *The Thinker*, and a long-necked Modigliani adorned Glenn's wall. Maroon and gold Indian bedspreads with tiny mirrors covered the two single beds. Patrick's wall had his most recent chalk drawings, close-ups of faces and reclining nudes. Glenn's tidy side of the closet held cool clothes from our older cousins. He and Pat would laugh hysterically when Glenn would pull out his old hand-me-downs from Patrick's side of the closet and say things like, "Now here's a handsome shirt!" When Glenn laughed, he threw back his head and opened his mouth as if trying to catch raindrops. I sat down on Pat's bed and nervously picked at a loose thread on the bedspread. "So, Mom says you're gonna move out soon," I said to Glenn. He was eighteen.

"I can't wait to live my own life." Glenn put down his book. "I'm not like all the other people here in San Leandro. You don't know it yet, but you're not either."

I picked at the bedspread some more. My stomach tightened at the thought of Glenn leaving.

Glenn took a small box from his nightstand and held it up. "Do you like this? Look closely."

An intricate design was painted around its perimeter.

"Elephants!" I exclaimed.

His almond-shaped blue eyes sparkled.

* * *

Everyone found his or her usual spots around the supper table. Our dinners had never been a surprise: Fridays were fish sticks or creamed tuna on toast while other weekdays were meat loaf, spaghetti, pork chops, beans, or stew. Saturdays were pot roast or roast beef, and Sundays had always been supper at Grandma's.

According to Mom, potatoes went with everything, so we had them every night along with some kind of mushy vegetable, canned fruit, and whole milk. Tonight's dinner was roast beef and gravy with mashed potatoes and peas. Mom's mashed potatoes weren't as tasty as Grandma's, which was good; otherwise, my vow of not eating them would be in serious jeopardy. These days, we didn't go to Grandma's house for Sunday supper much anymore; our lives had become complicated with homework and friends, while Grandma and Grandpa's failing health kept them from entertaining. Sometimes they'd come to our house for dinner, but that morning Grandma had said she thought they should stay home. Grandpa had become more disoriented lately, and Grandma had to be tired.

An extra chair had been added next to Glenn's place. He had invited a friend to dinner, and the two of them had listened to classical records upstairs. As Jack sat down at the table, Dad came into the kitchen. Now that I was more mature I called him Dad rather than Daddy.

Jack stood up by his chair and reached out his hand. "Nice to meet you, sir," he said. Jack wore tight blue jeans. His brown layered hair, worn below the ear, was thick and wiry but fluffy as though he had been in a deep sleep and just woken up. He had green eyes and curly lashes.

"Nice to meet you too, Jack. Good name," Dad said smiling impishly.

"So, Jack, Glenn says you two are thinking about getting an apartment together," Mom said, passing him the platter of sliced beef.

"I think I may have found a place this morning," Jack said. "It's a good size, and the natural lighting is lovely." Jack's voice was melodious with a hint of allergy stuffiness. Dad took an extra second to look from Jack to Glenn before planting his fork in the slice of roast beef.

"So, Jack, are you a student at San Francisco State, too?" Dad asked.

"Oh no, I graduated from the University of Montana a few years ago. I studied architecture. Now I work for the San Francisco Opera designing sets."

"Oh that must be wonderful, honey ... huh, Daddy?" Mom said brightly. Dad smiled tightly.

Later that night Dad went to the dining room to lower the temperature on the gauge for the night. Through the dark living room Dad saw Glenn and Jack, half clothed, embracing. When they saw Dad, they sat up and started a conversation. Glenn told me that Dad never spoke a word about it to him, or Mom, or anyone else. He wasn't one to share his feelings, and he avoided confrontation. But I imagine the scene was hard to forget.

* * *

"You've got your hands full with school, honey, let me bring dinner," Mom said to Glenn on the phone when he invited us over to his new place. Her offer was both kind and pragmatic: Glenn had once heated soup in its can in a pot on the stove, which blew the chicken noodles all over the walls.

Patrick was working at Jerry's Pancake House next to Jerry's Beef Burgers, so just Joan, Sue, and I sat together in the backseat as Dad inched across the bridge as though reluctant to cross the bay. My parents avoided San Francisco, unsettled by its pace—cars, trucks, and bicycles sharing the same lane, one-way streets, and people crowding the sidewalks. The rush of activity made Mom nervous and triggered Dad's migraines. Living only thirty minutes away, my parents almost never went there.

The bridge towers, like welcoming steel arms, pointed the way to the miraculous downtown buildings, some short and wide, others tall and narrow, stacked like the cans in my little-girl cupboard but with lights, looking like giant checkerboards. The Golden Gate Bridge was being enveloped in fog. Beyond the bridge were the ocean and the vast world beyond. I yearned for it.

All the windows were rolled up. I felt claustrophobic. Frank Sinatra sang "Strangers in the Night" on the radio.

"Mom, can you change the station?" I asked.

"But I love this song," Mom replied. Sue groaned. Joan pretended to put her finger down her throat. The song warbled on.

The directions to Glenn's place were on top of the waxed paper covering the spaghetti bowl in Mom's lap. Her cigarette waved as she signaled turns.

"Okay. Now go up a few streets and make a left on Market ..."

"Did Glenn say whether Jack was going to be there?" I asked.

"No, honey. He said he and Jack decided not to live together. He found some other roommates."

"Why? I like Jack."

"Honey, I'm not sure. Okay, Daddy, make a left here, on Castro. He said his place is right across from the hardware store." Lots of young men strolled along the street, some hand in hand, calling to one another; some of them were bare-chested in the warm weather. I stared in wonder. I'd never seen guys holding hands.

"Isn't that nice, a hardware store?" Mom pointed at Cliff's Hardware at Castro and Eighteenth, no doubt trying to divert Dad's attention. "Oh ... there's Glenn's place, Daddy—the big white house on the right."

When we rang the bell, Glenn popped out of a window. "I'll be right there!" Glenn opened the front door with beveled glass. He hugged Mom as she handed him the big pot of spaghetti wrapped in a towel and then hugged each of us girls. Dad smiled and patted Glenn on the arm awkwardly. "Hi, sport," he said with a tight smile.

Glenn, his face flushed, smiled briefly and looked away.

The ceiling was high with elaborately detailed crown molding. In the corner, a piece of a column that looked like a Roman ruin lay on its side. A multipaned window was balanced on the fireplace mantle.

Joan was in the bathroom. I followed. "Wow, this is nice," she said, taking in the octagonal black-and-white tiles on the floor and black towels hung in silver rings on the wall. I sniffed from a bottle on a beveled glass shelf above the toilet. It smelled just like Jack.

Glenn's roommates had classes that night. He poured each of us some Fanta orange drink. It was funny to have him as our host. He scooped spaghetti onto each of our plates as we sat down on the wooden crates around the table.

Mom held up her glass. "Here's to your freedom, honey." Mom's eyes danced happily. Dad held his glass high. Had the two of them ever felt this kind of freedom? They'd been married just a year after Daddy got home from the war. Baby followed baby until there were five of us kids in seven years. By that time, Mom and Dad had reached the ripe old age of twenty-eight. Neither of them seemed to want anything more than a safe world surrounded by those they loved. Unfortunately, Mom's illness made this an elusive goal.

So they looked on Glenn's independence as a good thing. And Glenn himself smiled radiantly. In time, the rest of us would follow his lead.

After dinner, Glenn played a Frank Sinatra album that he'd found at the recycled record store down the street. Mom took Dad's hand, and though self-conscious, Dad lifted his arm and spun her around. Mom had always been the best dancer of us all: smooth, precise, and right on beat. But as Dad swung her around, she stepped on his foot. "Honey, I think I may have lost my touch a little," she laughed. When the rest of us clapped, the two of them giggled like smitten teenagers.

Sue thumbed through the crate of albums on the floor next to the stereo. There, mixed in with Glenn's *Gypsy!* Mary Wells and *Black Orpheus* were Chopin, Rachmaninoff, and Ravel.

On our way home, as we drove up Castro toward Market, Jack came out of a used record store and crossed the street in front of us, heading in the direction of Glenn's place. We all saw him.

I knew Glenn and Jack were living together. I wondered if they walked down the street holding hands too. If Mom and Dad wondered the same thing, they didn't say it. The car was silent.

Chapter 6

❧

Bier with Pretzels

I was in Miss Cunningham's class drawing a geometric design in the left margin of my math scratch paper. If I could just get through the next few minutes, it would be recess. I'd stand with the girls, and no one would notice me staring at him. His name was Paul. Like Paul McCartney. "Bierwith is his last name, as in beer with pretzels," a classmate named Kim told me when he started walking her home and they soon became an item. His brown hair was, unlike mine, thick and wavy; his eyes were big and bright blue. ("Have you *seen* his long eyelashes?" Kim asked dreamily.) I had. Since the first day of school when Kim pointed him out, I'd been mesmerized.

The recess bell rang, and I hurried to join the girls next to the baseball diamond. The boys congregated near the basketball court. In those days, seventh grade was the last year of elementary school in the San Leandro school district. As sophisticated seventh graders, we were way too cool to do anything but stand around and talk when we went outside. Kim's womanly hips swayed when she walked over. She knew just how to pucker her lips after applying lip gloss. She scoffed at Bonnie and me when we marched arm in arm across the field. "You guys are embarrassing me," she'd say, "cut it out, or walk on the other side of the field." We stopped, mortified at our cluelessness.

Kim talked with Paul. I hated seeing the two of them standing so close. Later that day, the playground buzzed with the news: they'd broken up. "He's just too shy for me," Kim explained. "I'm seeing an eighth grader now. He's *so* much more mature."

Back in the classroom, Miss Cunningham's upper dentures visibly loosened from her gums in her rage. "Whoever took the blackboard erasers will get one week of detention," she promised. Her nose, always large, looked Toucan-ish on her angry red face.

It had to have been Roy. He was the only one who had the nerve. Roy had been my boyfriend off and on since second grade. Strangely, we both moved the same year from Oakland to this neighborhood. Now we were just friends. I smiled at him, and he jotted on a piece of paper, folded it, dropped it on the floor, and slyly kicked it my way.

Miss Cunningham's red Keds came nearer. She swooped up the folded paper. Then she read it out loud, enunciating each word with an exaggerated Southern twang, "You like Paul, don't you?" Thank God Paul was in a different class.

The heat rose from my feet, enveloping my shoulders, neck, and ears.

"Well, Miss Kennedy, since you and Roy have seen fit to disrupt the entire class, I think we all deserve an answer. Do you or don't you like *Paauulll?*"

I stared at my desk in mortified silence. After class, Bonnie stood watch in the girls' bathroom while I sobbed in a stall.

After school, as Bonnie and I walked morosely across the field, Roy ran up to us, breathless. "Have you seen the brick wall next to the playground?"

"Shut up!" I shouted. Him and his stupid note!

He laughed. "No, I swear. Someone wrote "Paul + Peggy" on the brick wall. Paul says he doesn't care. I think he likes you."

"You're lying." Bonnie and I kept walking. A cluster of boys brushed by. I glanced sideways. Paul. I cringed. *He's probably on his way to cross it out.* I kept my head down, hoping he wouldn't see me.

"Hi." His voice was deeper than I expected. I turned to see him smiling. I hadn't known he had braces. On him, they looked good.

"Hi," I said back, shyly. I could barely look at him much less talk to him. Bonnie dutifully walked in the middle and made conversation.

For the first month, we communicated through Bonnie, our interpreter. I wished we could walk to Bonnie's house and pretend it was mine. Bonnie never had to worry about bursting in on her mother having coffee with Jesus. Paul's mom was a schoolteacher. I was certain everything in his house was always in order. I'd heard his house was filled with Persian rugs and expensive artwork. What would he think when he saw the miniature pool table and boxes in our dining room? What if Mom was whooping around the house to the *Lone Ranger*? Paul would recoil and I would revert back to my former pudgy, bespectacled self.

My glasses were long gone from my headboard; I had buried them on a Santa Cruz beach the summer before. When Mom wearily suggested I needed another pair, I replied that I could see perfectly well without them. So what if I had to pull at the corners of my eyes to see the blackboard?

I wouldn't let him in my house. The three of us spent each day after school on my front lawn. In an effort to arrive at the house when everyone was inside, I feigned interest in flower plantings, oddly painted houses, anything to slow our pace home. One day, when Bonnie was sick and stayed home, my palms began to sweat as three o'clock approached. What could I possibly talk with him about?

We both stared at the sidewalk as we walked. Think of something! "What's your favorite color?"

"Definitely blue," he said too quickly. *Blue: just like Paul McCartney.* "What's yours?"

"Green: I like trees and stuff." I said. *Stupid answer!* He nodded. "Green's nice."

It was a start.

Rain poured that January. Paul and I leaned against the porch railing trying to get a Slinky to go down all the steps without stopping. Patrick opened the front door. "You guys are getting soaked. Paul, you're coming in."

"No!" I blurted.

Paul smiled gratefully. I followed him into the living room. "So, Paul, relax and dry out," Pat said and left the room.

I sat on the edge of the orange chair, and Paul sat on the green and black tweed one. Paul looked up at the beams. "Nice house," he smiled.

Then I saw it. Even with my blurry vision I could make it out: there in the dining room, under the miniature pool table next to the little pool cue, was a small brown turd. Pogo was getting old. We never knew where he was going to poop. I hurried to the octagon window next to the fireplace and made a big show of taking out one of the demitasse cups from the glass shelf to distract his attention.

The front door opened. "Well, look who's here! Hi, Paul— so nice to see you *in* the house, honey," Mom said shaking her umbrella on the front porch before putting it in the coat closet. "Oh, what beautiful eyelashes you have!"

Still talking, she scooped up the turd with a tissue. "You two are so cute I want to eat you up!" she smiled toothily before tapping the long ash of her cigarette on the turd and walking into the kitchen. I didn't dare meet Paul's eyes. For a second, I considered telling him about Mom's mental illness, but changed my mind. It would scare him away.

* * *

Patrick graduated from high school that June. That summer, he seemed intent on enjoying hanging out with his friends before they all left for college. Pat and his best friend Danny, who was tall and handsome with golden curls like the Archangel Gabriel in my holy card, hung out a lot at our house, to my delight. One night Pat caught Dan and Joan kissing in the hallway.

After Dan went home, Pat took Joan aside in the kitchen where she and I were making cookies. "Honey, he's a lot older than you," he warned. Joan was fifteen, and Dan, eighteen.

"I'm old enough to do what I want now, Pat," Joan replied with surprising steeliness. Like me, she usually listened to Patrick, now that Glenn was out of the house. Patrick knew it was useless to repeat his warning.

"God, I hope they're not having sex," I later overheard Pat say to Sue.

"Me, too," said Sue. "But I bet they are."

At that point, sex was way off my radar screen: after nearly a year of going steady, Paul and I had just gotten up the nerve to kiss.

* * *

Just before Patrick moved to a dorm at UC Santa Cruz later that summer, I convinced him to turn his bedroom over to me. I wanted my new room to be hip. I was tired of my headboard and okay, maybe even a little tired of the Paul McCartney photos I'd clipped from a Beatles fan magazine and stuck to my wall. It wasn't that long since I had pored over the vital statistics: "Likes: fish and chips; Weight: 73 kilos; Height: 5' 11"; dislikes: mean people." As a kid, when I went downstairs I made sure to hit the lowered part of the ceiling just above the second stair to ensure that I would one day marry Paul McCartney.

* * *

A flickering light came from the den as I made my way to the bathroom late one night a couple of weeks later. Mom sat on the floor near the television stroking Pogo's head. Mom didn't watch television—she found it boring—yet she was watching Johnny Carson.

"Mom?" I asked quietly.

She turned. She'd been crying—something I'd never seen her do. Anything Mom did out of the ordinary made me worry. I watched her eyes.

"He's gone, Peg." Joining her on the floor in tears next to Pogo's still body, I realized that Mom also existed outside my anxiousness; that she was a real human being with a wide range of emotion. Mom never yelled unless she was heading for a breakdown. At those times, she picked fights with Dad over why the faucet was leaky or the kitchen stool wobbled. Usually by the next day, Mom's eyes would be jumpy; and she'd say something like everyone in the world was being poisoned by pepper. But what if, on that first day, Mom was simply having a bad day and being testy? Didn't she have the right to express how she felt without everyone analyzing her tone while they worriedly studied her eyes? How many times had she held back her emotions for fear of being carted off to Napa or Agnews, or at the very least, of alarming us kids? It can't be comfortable to have your family always watching to see if you're going crazy again.

Chapter 7

꒰꒱

It's Alright, Ma

September, 1967

Sue's corner of our room was a country unto itself. She prided
herself on reading a wide range of philosophers and poets. The
wall next to her bed was covered in neatly written quotes taken
from her favorite books. In the event that we had to move, Sue,
like the prehistoric cave painters of Lascaux, would leave behind
her wall scratchings as evidence she'd been there.

Sue sat cross-legged on her mattress, pen poised in one hand,
ready to write in her leather portfolio, cigarette in the other. She
smoked openly in our room. Mom and Dad pretended not to
notice. Bob Dylan's "It's Alright, Ma, I'm Only Bleeding" played
on the stereo. An African wind chime made from what looked
like long white teeth hung from the ceiling at the end of Sue's
bed; when the wind came through the open window, the teeth

clunked like hollow spears. Sue's *Blue Boy* poster hung above her bed, a calming influence on the tormented corner. Bookshelves on cinder blocks held dozens of books. I was sure Sue had read each one at least once. The stereo, a turntable with two speakers, was under the window to the right of her bed. On top of one of the speakers was a stack of 45s. Next to it was a crate that held all of our albums, an eclectic mix of everything from Dylan, the Rolling Stones, and every existing Beatles LP to movie albums from *To Kill a Mockingbird; Hello, Dolly;* and *West Side Story.*

"Thank God it's my last year of high school," Sue said to the bathroom mirror as we girls dressed for school. Her habit of chewing on her tongue in concentration through the years had caused her front teeth to protrude slightly, making her smile look especially confident.

It was my first day of junior high and eighth grade. I took my new skirt and blouse out of the closet while Joan went into the bathroom to brush her teeth. I listened to the two of them chatting.

"Today, my dear sister," Sue continued rakishly, "is going to be interesting." "And why is that?" Joan asked through a mouth full of foaming Crest.

"Don has given me a little something." Sue replied. Patrick had been adamant that Sue avoid Don. "He's a stoner, Sue. All that group does is get high. Be careful." Sue had seen Don, anyway. Don had soft brown curls, green eyes, a receding hairline, and a boyish face.

We three ended up in the kitchen at the same time. Sue grabbed an apple and rushed toward the back door. Mom gazed absently out the window from her place at the table. "Have a good day, Sue Sue," she called.

"Thanks, Mom, I will," Sue impishly replied.

That day after school I searched Joan's sewing machine table for safety pins for the skirt I planned to wear the next day. Safety pins had become my instant tailor: the more weight I lost, the more pins I needed. I wasn't interested in learning how to sew, and Joan wasn't interested in taking in my clothes. Mom would have done it, but she was at work all day and never slowed down long enough to ask. It was easier to pin them and be done with it.

At bedtime Sue dragged herself up the stairs, made a beeline to her mattress in the corner, and climbed into her sleeping bag. "*Brrrr*," she said, thrusting her arm out to pick up her pen and portfolio off the floor.

I pretended to inspect a skirt pattern that lay across Joan's sewing table.

Sue stopped writing. "Peg—did you want to ask me something?"

I hesitated. "Um … I just wondered if your day was okay."

"Peg, do you know anything about drugs?"

"Kinda," I responded coolly.

"I took some mescalin. Have you ever heard of Aldous Huxley?" I shook my head. "He wrote a book called *The Doors of Perception: Heaven and Hell* that describes how mescalin alters your consciousness. I have it here if you want to read it." She lifted the book for me to see.

I was nonchalant. "No, that's okay."

"In answer to your question, I had an amazing day. But now I'm freezing, and my head feels like it's been bludgeoned with a hammer. Could you do me a huge favor and get me a cup of hot water with lemon and honey?" She gave me a half-Cheshire cat smile.

When I returned with the hot drink, Sue was asleep so I made a place on her bookshelf and set the cup down. I brought the Aldous Huxley book to my room. If I needed to rescue her, I better find out where she was going.

That night, Dad was working, so Mom walked over to meet her friend Bea at a neighborhood bar. Later, I heard a car and peeked out. A tall man with dark hair came around to let Mom out. Mom smiled the way she did in front of the mirror after putting on lipstick. The man watched her walk up our front stairs. My stomach jumped. I never asked Mom who the man was and didn't mention him to my siblings. Maybe she just needed a ride.

* * *

Although I adored all my siblings, Joan was my role model. Her face was slender and oval shaped, while mine was rectangular, which made it look fat; her freckles were faded, while mine were obvious. But she looked the most like me, was closest to me in age, and was more self-assured than anyone I knew. So when Joan signed up to learn Russian, I did, too. I was twelve, almost thirteen, and starting eighth grade at Bancroft Jr. High School. Joan was fifteen and a half, starting tenth grade at San Leandro High School. Bancroft was for eighth and ninth graders, San Leandro for tenth, eleventh, and twelfth graders.

She had raved for two years about Mr. Stern, the kind but sometimes befuddled teacher who'd managed, during that Cold War period, to talk the school district into letting him teach Russian to students in junior and senior high school.

So when Joan told me one night what had happened in her Russian class that day, I could picture the whole thing: Mr. Stern in his baggy corduroy pants and sport coat with suede elbow patches writing verb declensions on the blackboard; Joan, nauseous, watching his right hand move up and down while his left hand pushed up his wire rim glasses. Joan raised her hand. "Da, Ivana Ivanovna?"

Joan blurted out: "I'm gonna be sick!" She ran to the bathroom just in time to heave into the toilet.

She didn't tell me until later that she'd hoped to God it was the flu.

* * *

Helicopters wicketed, and guns pattered on the television in my parents' bedroom as the Vietnam War dominated every night's newscast. One night when I entered her bedroom Joan's face was buried in her pillow and her shoulders shook as Danny sat on her bed and helplessly stroked her hair. Afraid of being drafted into the army, Danny had enlisted for four years in the navy. Danny was Joan's first and only boyfriend, and now he was leaving. He seemed surprised by her tears. He obviously hadn't been around when she watched *Lassie*.

Joan told me later that she knew it was coming. Pat and Glenn hadn't been drafted only because they were in four-year colleges. "Danny will be safer on a ship," she said, more to convince herself than me.

* * *

October, 1967

The smell of tomato and oregano seeped into my bedroom. I lay on the Indian bedspread Pat had bought me for my birthday, reading Gandhi's *Autobiography*, one of many books Pat and Glenn had left behind, while listening to the Moody Blues. I planned to go to India someday.

Mom's approaching heels clicked rigidly against the hardwood floor of the hallway. Normally, she put on slippers when she got home, but today she kept her heels on as though she had somewhere else to go. With a sick feeling in the pit of my stomach, I turned off "Nights In White Satin."

Mom sat down on my bed. Tired of fussing with her hair, she'd taken to wearing a brown wig she had styled at Spiro's Aphrodite Salon, not far from our house. Her cold hand squeezed mine so tight I could feel the separation between her engagement and wedding rings. "Peg, how would you feel about moving to San Francisco?"

"*What?*" I asked, horrified. I loved "The City," as everybody called it, but I certainly didn't want to live there with my parents.

"Maybe we could find a little place near Glenn."

The thought that Mom might want a shot at freedom and adventure didn't occur to me then. As far as I could see, she was once again losing her grip on reality.

"You guys don't even *like* San Francisco. It makes you nervous," I pointed out. My heart raced.

"Sure we do, honey. Just think: we could go to plays and the symphony …"

"Mom, *listen to me.*" I tried to focus on her eyes, but they were dancing. "You don't like going to plays, and you *never* listen to classical music."

"Oh, honey, don't be silly. I *love* classical music."

Had Dad really agreed to this? Maybe he had played along, in the hope that agreeing would delay his having to make the call to institutionalize her. My chest tightened as I thought of Paul. We'd certainly break up if I moved. Tears formed in my eyes.

"Oh, Lord." Mom said with exasperation. She abruptly left the room. She must have felt trapped in a circumscribed life, without anything to look forward to but spaghetti for dinner, propped-up pillows against the headboard to watch television shows she didn't like, and a husband who didn't like going out.

Had she stopped taking her medication? We'd all become experts at detecting the progressive signs of Mom's illness: First day: she'd become argumentative, usually with Daddy, but also with us kids. She'd claim, for instance, that a teacup was red when it was blue, and challenge us to prove her wrong. If we tried, she'd make us feel that we had betrayed her. Glenn often sided with her against Daddy (she always blamed her hospitalizations on Daddy because he would call for the ambulance to take her) but Pat challenged. Her pupils would dilate and her eyes would become restless. Second day: her words would run together as thoughts raced through her mind. Often, she'd grow fond of a certain phrase (it could be anything) and she'd repeat it wherever she went whether it made sense or not. Once she glommed on to the French phrase "Voulez-vous coucher avec moi," which she said in thanks to the butcher after he'd handed her a pound of ground round. She moved faster around the house, picking up things and putting them somewhere else for no reason; her laugh became shrill and cackly. Her eyes would move back and forth rapidly. Once Mom had declared that Christ was sitting on the end of her bed drinking coffee. "Oh, Peg, he's *soooo* handsome," she told me woozily. Was it right to lust after Jesus? I winced, but felt compelled to ask: "Does he take cream and sugar?"

Mom nodded eagerly. "Both!" Later that night, Dad convinced her to go back on her medication.

On the third day, typically, she talked with people that weren't there; her face expressionless; her speech, though slower, contained no terms of endearment, in fact, she began to speak like a guest in a house full of people she didn't know (and didn't like). Sometimes she became frightened, convinced that we were conspiring against her. The fact that soon after she behaved like this she would get taken away probably reinforced this feeling.

In the end, Mom's doctors decided she was less schizophrenic than severely manic depressive (later called Bipolar Disorder) with "Rapid Cycling," in which a person experiences more than four mood swings within a twelve-month period. This meant that at any given time if she went off her medication, likely as not, she would cycle (usually over a three-day period) into a severe psychotic episode. Sometimes, since it was an inexact science that depended to some extent on her hormones, Mom could begin cycling even while on medication, and would have to be hospitalized to have it adjusted. In either case, she seemed to be institutionalized about once every two years, and they would keep her at one of the three state hospitals (I don't know why they chose one over the other at any given time)—Napa, Stockton or Agnews—for three to six months, giving her electroshock therapy and drugs to get her back to normal again. Sometimes Mom stopped taking her pills when the medication made her feel better, so she thought she didn't need it anymore. The side effects of the pills could be unpleasant, including tremors, constipation, dry mouth, foggy-headedness, and blurry vision. The drugs often made Mom lethargic, which is why she spent so much time lying on her bed. She probably also liked feeling her energy—albeit manic energy—return when she stopped taking the pills. I haven't ruled out that she also did it to get attention, especially when she couldn't legally be involuntarily locked up anymore. If she *had* stopped taking her pills, and we detected it early (and convinced her to start again) our lives could go back to our version of normal.

When lithium was approved by the FDA for treatment of manic depression in 1970, it worked well for her. In the 1980s, shots became available that she could take once every two weeks. With the shots there was no doubt she was getting her medication. By that time, she was relieved as the rest of us to have something that kept her regulated.

In the late 1960s, however, mental patients did not control their own destinies. Since Dad had to make the call, Mom blamed him for her institutionalizations: he was both her husband and her warden. Though Mom's resentment toward Dad erupted only when she was being taken away—when she was not in her right mind—I wondered to what extent it smoldered beneath the surface when she was.

One Friday evening, though Daddy was off work, Mom asked Bea to meet her for a drink. Sue was out with a friend. Dateless, Joan and I sat on Sue's mattress, backs against the wall, eyes directed at a movie on the black-and-white set on its rolling table near our feet. Danny was on a ship somewhere, and Paul was on restriction for having come home the weekend before at 2:00 a.m. from a bus expedition the two of us took to see

Santana at the Fillmore. (Dad had been working and Mom had been asleep, so I slipped into bed undetected).

Joan, tucked inside Sue's sleeping bag, picked up a clump of the chocolate chip cookie dough we'd just made, removed all the chips, and then put them to the side of the bowl and took a bite. Luckily our tastes in this regard differed: she liked the dough and I preferred the chips. I scooped up the chips and threw them in my mouth. Having become a vegetarian after reading Gandhi's autobiography, I refused to eat the fish sticks Mom served earlier at dinner. "Egetha, you're getting as skinny as a rail," Mom complained, as she'd plunked down two ears of corn on my plate. Even though all my clothes needed pinning now, I still thought I was fat. Afraid of putting on weight, I'd eaten only one of the two ears of corn. But somehow, candy always made it onto even the most stringent of my diets.

We could hear bits and pieces of Mom and Dad's bedroom conversation.

"If you don't want to come that's fine, Jack."

"The doctor said you're not supposed to drink, Barbara."

"Here we go again. I'm sick to death of not being able to do anything. I can't drink, can't talk too fast, I can't even get angry without everyone thinking that I've gone crazy again."

I couldn't hear Dad's response.

"I'm going out," Mom said. Her heels clicked against the floor down the hall and across the foyer. The door closed hard.

After the movie, I peeked in on Dad, who lay immobile in his dark bedroom. Poor Daddy: another migraine.

A loud bump against the hallway wall woke me up in the middle of the night. My parents' bedroom door opened.

"Jack, I want a separation," I heard my mother slur.

"Barb, you've been drinking. Let's talk in the morning."

"I know what I'm saying." A long pause was followed by the clunk of tossed shoes. The bed squeaked as Mom plopped herself down. "I want you to move to your mother's for a while." Her words were clearer now. I peeked through the crack of my door.

Mom and Dad faced each other on the bed. Dad was pale. I was sure his migraine was flaring.

"So, Jack, what do you think?"

"What do *I* think?" he asked, crossing his arms as his eyes narrowed. "I think you're getting sick again."

"*I'm FINE, Jack!*" Mom shouted. Her eyes, though angry, were still. "*I need this right now, Jack,*" she pleaded. Though emphatic, she sounded normal.

Dad hung up his shirt and kept his back turned. "Do I really have any choice?" He was going to go along with this!

The next morning Joan doodled on the newspaper, her toast untouched in front of her on the kitchen table. I told her what I had overheard and asked her what we should do. "Mom and Dad need each other too much to stay apart. Don't worry about it," she said as she colored glasses on a man's photo. I wasn't convinced and carried a lump of worry with me about it wherever I went. And Joan was distracted by her own worries.

The following Saturday morning Dad was at the front door, uniform on a hanger, suitcase next to him on the floor. Sue, Joan, and I surrounded him sadly. My father's eyes were wet as he picked up his suitcase. "Okay, sports. Take good care of your mother." It never occurred to him to tell us to take care of ourselves. He must have trusted that we were doing a good enough job of that already. I wished I shared his confidence in us. My brothers were busy at school, and Sue was acting wild—staying out late with friends and then stumbling into bed; missing school; and hanging out with Don's friends, a couple of whom were known to fight with knives and chains and sell drugs in the park. The only thing I felt I could control was what I ate, and I was running out of safety pins. Thank God I had Joan.

* * *

A couple of weeks later, I almost stepped in a glob of what looked like thick berry Jell-O on the doormat as I came in the house after school. A trail of blood led to the bathroom. Luckily, Paul had a track meet. It was as if Mom *wanted us to know* when she was having her period. A few years earlier as she signed a permission slip for me to watch a movie on menstruation, Mom said somberly, "This is important, honey." I grabbed the slip and dashed from the room before she had a chance to say anything more. Eew! Who wanted to hear about womanhood and babies?

Now Mom's womanhood was all over the floor. I scooped a handful of paper napkins from the kitchen and started wiping. But the more blood I cleaned up, the more I found. When I thought I got it all, I mopped the floor.

I tapped on the bathroom door. "Mom?" No one answered. I knocked. "Hello? Mom?" No answer again. My heart beat faster. Mom wasn't usually home until five o'clock. It was only four. Someone was in there.

I turned to see Joan's book bag lying in the doorway of the den across from the bathroom ... *Fastidious Joan. Oh my God.* "Joan?" I asked. I pounded on the door. No response. I tried the door: locked, of course. Everyone in our family locked the door—a person needed to have some privacy *somewhere*.

"JOAN!" I screamed, pounding again.

"God, what a mess," came a voice that sounded vaguely like Joan's.

I kept knocking, afraid that if I stopped she would stop answering. "Peg, I'm okay," Joan said tiredly through the door. Her voice was small and strained. I started to sob.

"Peg! I'm okay," she said through the door in a stronger voice. "I had an abortion. I'm bleeding a lot. I think I passed out." She must have looked in the mirror. "Oh my God, I'm as white as a sheet."

I sat down on the floor and leaned against the wall next to the bathroom. "You went to *Mexico?*" I asked incredulously. I'd heard people went there to have abortions. Just this morning, we'd sat across from each other at breakfast eating Sugar Smacks. How had she gotten there and back so fast?

Joan's laughter briefly poked through her exhaustion. "No, Hayward." Hayward was just ten minutes away.

"Oh," I laughed and added. "Are you okay?"

"I think so. I went to this skuzzy apartment. Old newspapers piled everywhere, peeling wallpaper. The guy was not a doctor. Sarah drove me home, but I told her not to come in."

"Did you tell Mom?"

"No. She would have wanted me to keep it."

"Do you want me to help you clean up?"

She sighed. "No, I can handle it. If I change my mind, I'll let you know."

Joan emerged a half hour later, frail and drawn, a bath towel wrapped around her waist. The skirt she'd made was now just a bloody wad shoved into the wastebasket she carried in her hand. I shivered. Sensible Joan had gotten pregnant and had a dangerous abortion. Who was left to look out for me? Who would be my role model?

Later that evening, I called Paul to see how his track meet had gone. His words calmed me.

Chapter 8

☙❧

Crash Landing

Dad asked us kids to meet him at our house on a Saturday morning. No one knew why. I sat at the table across from Glenn and Pat, whose cigarettes billowed smoke from ashtrays while they scanned the *Oakland Tribune*. The smoke created a fog around the three of us.

Dad nervously fingered the bills Mom had given him. It was strange to see him acting like a visitor, standing awkwardly in the kitchen next to the counter, as though he had no seat at the table. "Come sit down, Daddy," Patrick said. Dad just shook his head. His shirt puffed out like a parachute tucked into his baggy pants. His thinning hair was a whiter shade of gray. Living in Grandma's house had turned his skin the sallow color of buttery mashed potatoes. He smelled of Old Spice, the cologne that he only splashed on when he went out.

Joan came in. "Hi, Daddy." She took a step back. "Have you lost weight?" She voiced things I couldn't bring myself to.

Dad shrugged. Sue, who preferred to smoke alone, came in from the back porch, patted Dad's arm, and sat down.

The smell of hair spray wafted in, and we heard the sound of Mom's heels as she walked down the hall from her bedroom to the front door where the screen door opened and closed.

Dad said nothing. Sue pulled the leather-bound address book from the alcove under the phone and set it on the table. The book, once a testament to Mom's excellent handwriting and now filled with drawings, doodles, and funny remarks had become our bible of boredom. A few years earlier, Mom had innocently entered her friend Jean Parker's name and address in Mohawk, California, with a note next to it that read, "Mohawk, near Quincy." Now, next to Lou Parson's name under Jean Parker's in Glenn's handwriting was: "newly residing at Mohawk, near Quincy." Below Lou Parson, next to Dad's friend Don Patterson's address in Sue's handwriting was "tragically cut down at the intersection of Mohawk near Quincy." Continuing down the page, next to the name Amelia Pryce, a friend of Mom's we'd never met, was a drawing courtesy of Patrick of a bespectacled old woman with buck teeth in a feathered hat: Poor Amelia.

Dad stubbed his Camel out. "So I guess you're all wondering why I brought you here today." We laughed, wanting him to relax.

He sighed and rubbed his forehead as his mouth crumpled. "There's no easy way to say this." He let out a breath, and his chest appeared concave. He looked sideways at us, his mouth a straight line. "Your mother's pregnant, and I'm not the father."

All five of us put our hands over our mouths. It would have been comical, if anyone was in a mood to laugh. We said nothing.

"I'll be right back." Dad pushed away from the counter and walked out the kitchen door into the hall. The bathroom door closed. He was giving us a chance to absorb the news without him in the room.

"Good Lord," Glenn said.

Pat covered his face and shook his head. He let out a nervous laugh. "Second that."

"So that's why Mom's been so tired," Joan said. She was always the observant one.

"Do you think she wants to keep it?" Sue asked.

My father was back. "Dad," Patrick asked, "Have you decided how you and Mom are going to handle this? I mean ... are we going to keep the baby?"

"Does Mom want to keep it?" Joan asked.

"I think we should, I mean ... we could make it one of us," Glenn said.

Dad closed his eyes and gripped the counter with both hands as though his legs were about to collapse. When he turned, his face was purple like it had just taken a heavy punch. "What about me? What if *I* don't want to keep it?" Dad said. He spun on his heel, and a minute later we heard the screen door bang after him, too. Since early childhood, we had defended our mother, in our minds if not to the world. To blame her was to deny her sickness and all that we had lived through as a result of it. Blaming her was next to impossible. But defending Mom had never meant siding against Daddy—until now.

* * *

Mom and Dad agreed that Mom would stay with us girls through the end of the year and then move to an apartment before her pregnancy showed (Mom didn't want the neighbors gossiping, and Dad didn't want to have to move again). She would stay there until she had the baby and then give it up for adoption.

But I wanted to keep it. I could learn how to put on its diapers and teach it how to say "brush my hair" like my old Chatty Cathy doll that was missing its head ever since I twisted it off. I could hold the baby when it cried and teach it to walk so it could go to Quik Stop with me to get candy. We could lie and say one of our cousins had a baby and couldn't keep it. But Daddy would never agree. It wasn't his, and he didn't want it. And Mom wasn't going to fight him over it. Her brush with adventure had led her straight to being pregnant. Now she wouldn't even have a baby to show for it.

After Mom had the baby, she'd move home again. But after all that disagreeing, it didn't seem to me as though Mom and Dad could ever see eye to eye again.

My list of secrets and lies was growing. One afternoon Paul and I lay on my backyard lawn holding hands and finding imaginary creatures in the clouds above when Paul said, "I haven't seen your dad in a while."

"He's been working a lot of extra hours at the firehouse," I said quickly.

Mom often went in late to work because of morning sickness. I'd hear her in the morning throwing up in the toilet, then I'd hear the heavy clunk of the toilet lid. In November, she was laid off. She seemed relieved; she had probably dreaded the prospect of feigning excitement at work over the fact that she was pregnant. That Thanksgiving, Mom claimed that dressing a turkey would make her gag and instead served tamales on her big turkey platter. No one complained. It didn't seem much like Thanksgiving without Dad there anyway.

My parents must have agreed to trade holidays, because we spent Christmas at Grandma's with Dad. It had been awhile since we'd all been there. Not many years before, Mom's mental state was the only changeable thing in our lives. Now, change seemed to be the only thing we could rely on.

Though weak from a recent illness, Grandma managed to fix roast beef, mashed potatoes, and gravy. She'd been sick in the hospital, and Dad and Uncle Jim were taking care of Grandpa, who was getting more forgetful by the day. I assumed Dad was doing the cooking since I'd never seen Uncle Jim even close to the stove. Were they living on scrambled eggs and apple fritters?

"Darlin' put some meat on those bones," she said as she piled mashed potatoes on my plate. Now that we kids were older, we sat at Grandma and Grandpa's kitchen table with the adults. I moved my potatoes around my plate to make it look like I'd eaten them. Uncle Jim started to sing: "K-E-double N-E-D-Y spells Kennedy, Kennedy... ." Dad shook his head. "Not tonight, Jim," he said.

In January, Mom moved to an apartment in Alameda, and Dad moved back home. I told Paul that Mom was out of town visiting friends. I didn't know what I'd tell him if Mom decided to keep the baby and stay in Alameda.

* * *

May, 1968

Although we girls kept trying to visit Mom in Alameda, she always found a reason to cancel: she had a cold and didn't want us to catch it or she didn't want us to drive all that way (all of twenty minutes) and get stuck in traffic. It didn't take long to figure out that she was embarrassed by her situation and we were doing her a favor by not visiting. But we wanted to see her. One Saturday in early May, the three of us showed up on her doorstep. She lived in a two-story apartment with gray siding built in the 1950s.

I rang the doorbell. The door unlocked, and Mom's head peeked around. "*Yeeeeessssss?*" she said, grinning her big toothy Mother Rabbit smile. When she opened the door all the way, we gasped. Her stomach was huge! We all laughed as we tried to wrap our arms around her to give her a hug. It was easy to see that she was overjoyed that we had come.

Mom walked like Uncle Jack, her stomach leading the rest of her body to the living area, where a sofa bed lay open. Beside it was her nightstand from home. Atop it was a picture of our family standing on our front lawn one Easter Sunday years before. We girls wore matching dresses with flowered hats; the boys, slacks and white shirts. Mom and Dad smiled broadly behind us. At home, Mom had never been one to hang pictures of our family, thinking perhaps that it was too self-centered. Ella Fitzgerald sang a song about tiskets and taskets on the radio as Mom offered us a cup of coffee from the pot on her gold-speckled countertop, her hand trembling.

"So how are you feeling, Mom?" Sue asked.

"Good. I'm feeling really good, Sue-Sue," Mom said with a tired smile. Her manic tone had given way to a settled quietness, which was surprising considering she had gone off her Thorazine so as not to hurt the baby. Her pregnant hormones seemed to be stronger than her mental illness.

Mom sat down on her bed. Sue fluffed up the pillows, and Mom leaned back.

"Do you want me to get you anything at the store?" Joan asked. She was agitated, pacing. I'm sure it occurred to her that her baby would have been due at the same time as Mom's. Had she shuddered at the idea of the two of them spooning pablum into their babies' mouths at side-by-side high chairs?

I knew one thing: I wasn't having sex until I was eighteen and on the pill.

"I could use some milk and bread. You sure you don't mind, Joanie?"

"I'm sure," Joan replied, but her look said, "Anything to get out of here."

Joan left and the room was quiet. Mom looked from Sue to me. "I'm sorry this happened, girls."

"We're okay, Mom," Sue said.

Had I been younger, I would have asked when she was going to come home. Had she been pregnant with Dad's baby, I would have asked if I could feel it kick. As it was, I kept quiet. I didn't want to know this baby—it wasn't going to be ours. So I sat, my hands under me, not knowing what to do or say, but happy to be near my mother.

A couple of weeks later, Mom delivered a healthy baby boy. He was given up for adoption. She was not allowed to hold him. I imagined her standing at the nursery window watching him breathe tiny baby breaths under his blue blanket and trying not to think of names for him. And then a nurse coming to take her back to her room, kind, but firm, and perhaps mystified—a married woman giving up her child.

Dad brought Mom home a couple of days later. We tiptoed around her, trying not to see the sadness in her eyes. Mom's doctor increased her dosage of medication, which made her sleep most of the time. Dad made sure she always had a fresh pot of coffee on her nightstand and her robe at the foot of her bed. Mom accepted his pampering, grateful that he'd begun to forgive her.

I couldn't help but wonder how it would have felt to be an older sister. Mom volunteered that the father was a doctor with red hair, but we couldn't get anything else out of her. When, years later, we asked Mom if she wanted us to find the child (then a young man) she said that if he was interested, he'd try to find us, and that it wouldn't be right for us to try and find him. We never looked for him.

* * *

It was still light outside when Mom crawled into bed one evening in early June. When the phone rang, I lay on my bed working on an essay. Finally, after the sixth ring, Mom picked up. Her bed creaked as she rolled over and yelled upstairs, "Susie, honey, it's for you."

"I've got to finish this poem," Sue hollered.

Moments later, Mom stood at the foot of the stairs. "Susie, come to the phone, honey. Sally's crying."

Sue clattered down the stairs and picked up the receiver. Seconds later, she froze and her eyes went blank.

"Susie, what is it?" Mom said.

"Don."

Within minutes, there was a knock on the front door and Sally rushed in, her hair uncombed, wailing, "I can't believe Don did this. Goddamned acid!"

Mom and I exchanged wary glances.

"Sally, what happened?" Mom asked.

"Don took some LSD and decided he could fly. He jumped out of a three-story building downtown. He's in intensive care."

Sally and Sue sped off in Sally's car. Sally was dating Don's best friend Paul, so being with Don meant that Sue became best friends with Sally. Sally had waist-long brown hair, laughed often, spoke in a deep voice like Lauren Bacall, and sped around town in her cool green Morris Minor car.

A few hours later, Sally called to tell us Don was dead.

For the next few weeks, Sue lay on her mattress, not listening to music or reading, just staring at the ceiling. Years later, Sue told me that after Don's death, she'd made a habit of borrowing Mom's medication. It made her sleep a lot. She slinked downstairs to eat at night like the zombies in *Night of the Living Dead*. If we asked her something, we'd get a blank stare and then she'd turn away, so Joan and I would make up answers for her. Joan: "Hey, Sue, Whaddya say I bring all your albums to Rasputin's and see how much they'll give me for them? What was that? I can keep all the money? God, you're generous!" When Sue skipped her high school graduation ceremony Mom took it in stride, but when she took no steps to apply for college, Mom called Glenn.

"I don't care what you study, Sue," Glenn said earnestly. He sat on a chair next to Sue's bed later that night while Mom, Joan, and I peeked in from the hall. "Poetry or textiles, or the effects of reading Rilke while hanging upside down from a tree. Just use your brain, and thank God you've got one!"

Two weeks later, Sue shocked us all by signing up for classes at a junior college in Los Altos on the San Francisco peninsula. Even more surprising, she found a job as a live-in nanny with one of her professors. When she left for Los Altos at the end of July, I was certain she'd be home in a week. Sue had never been fond of babysitting, and she played the mother role with her younger siblings only when she had no other choice.

I was wrong. Going to school and spending time with her little charges—taking them to the park and drawing pictures with them—seemed to bring Sue back. When she called and asked me to send her leather writing portfolio, I wrapped it up and took it to the post office myself, so relieved that I felt like skipping.

Chapter 9

꒰꒱

A Signed 8 x 10 Glossy

Christmas, 1968

Paul had come over, and now handed me a small package wrapped
unevenly in Christmas paper. Inside was a necklace with a St.
Christopher medal on it to match the one I'd given him. I smiled
as he fastened it at the back of my neck. We'd started off slowly
enough—waiting for almost a year to kiss because we were both
so shy—but once we got over that hurdle, at parties we would
find a comfortable place to sit and never come up for air. Once
Paul was chewing gum while we were making out, and it ended
up tangled in my hair. We were *that* wrapped up in each other.
I twirled the curls at the nape of his neck (curls were foreign to
me—the only ones I'd ever known had been manufactured from
a box of Toni Home Permanent).

I was more relaxed now with Paul around my family. He seemed to like them. But in my excitement at seeing him, I forgot about the Santa hats and beards and even about the lacy underwear on Daddy's head. I guided Paul into the living room.

"Hi, Paul," Mom's voice muffled through her beard as Dad snatched the panties from his head. I was certain Paul saw them. In unison, all the other Santas chortled, beards jiggling, shoulders shaking.

Paul's eyes widened as he laughed. He didn't miss a beat. "Where's my hat and beard?"

Sue had come prepared with an extra Santa hat and beard. She tossed them to Paul, and we both put ours on. With his big blue eyes and long eyelashes, Paul was the best looking Santa of all. His eyes wandered to the Christmas tree. I thought of diverting his attention, but didn't. "*Ho Ho Ho!*" he chuckled when he saw my first-grade picture. (We had a custom of hanging one another's ugliest pictures on the tree and mine, with two gaping holes at the front of my mouth, crooked pink glasses, and a scraggly ponytail, was the funniest of all.)

* * *

My father's parents were failing. Grandpa died a few days after Christmas, and Grandma went just months later. By the time Grandpa passed away, most of the father that Dad had known had already disappeared. Grandpa grew more forgetful with age and often stood on his back porch looking at his yard scratching his head. Daddy told us Grandpa had been trying to grow a lawn in his backyard ever since Dad was a kid but had only grown weeds. He mowed them anyway. In contrast, Grandma was her warm, vibrant self to the end, which must have made her passing that much more difficult for my father, and definitely, for us. Near the end, Grandma and Grandpa were hospitalized at the same time just one floor away from one another, but neither one wanted Dad to tell the other that they were hospitalized—they didn't want to worry each other.

Dad was teary-eyed and quiet when he popped his head in my room early Good Friday morning (Grandma must have planned that one) to tell me that Grandma had died. I don't remember Grandpa's funeral, but Grandma's was a big event: Mom and Dad took us shopping for just the right attire for the funeral. The funeral was to be at St. Elizabeth's, their alma mater, and they wanted to make a good impression. I chose a charcoal gray suit (my first suit ever—I loved it) and a hat trimmed with gray ribbon to match. I remember walking down the aisle after the funeral mass, smiling at the people in the packed pews. I'm sure they were bewildered at my expression, but I was happy for my grandmother. She was right where she'd always wanted to be.

I hardly ate a thing at the reception back at the house. The list of what I would eat had shortened: Grape Nuts, apples, and red or black licorice. Now in ninth grade, I was skinny and happy about it. I finally liked how I looked. Though often cold, I could bundle up in sweaters and socks and still look thin. Paul seemed to like it that he could put his hands all the way around my waist. Mom grew more worried and enlisted Joan's help.

"Peg, how much do you weigh?" Joan asked me one morning as I ate my breakfast bowl of Grape Nuts (I ate another bowl for dinner). I was pleased that she'd noticed.

"Eighty-five," I said proudly.

"*Eighty-five?* Peg, how tall are you, five-five? I'm five-four, for God's sakes, and I weigh twenty-five pounds more than you. You need to start eating more."

I said I would, but I knew she was just jealous.

I wasn't happy, though. Something was wrong, and one day when Paul was hanging out with friends after school, I walked through a light rain that made the sidewalks to church shimmer. Once inside, I inhaled the incense and crossed myself with holy water before taking a pew behind the only other person there, who was an elderly woman wearing a black mantilla. I guess I was thinking that, as in a restaurant, it was the only section open. Unlike the bland modern windows at St. Louis Bertrand's Church that we attended as kids, the stained-glass windows of the Church of the Assumption in San Leandro depicted the Stations of the Cross in graphic detail, with blood under the Crown of Thorns and on Christ's wrists and feet as he hung on the cross. Grandma would have approved. I felt at home. I pulled out Mom's black rosary beads, which I now always carried in my purse, and I launched into a silent recitation of the Act of Contrition, Our Father, and a whole host of Hail Marys.

Feeling the eyes of the elderly woman on me as she hobbled past me toward the door, I looked up. She pointed to a priest waiting for us to leave so he could lock up. I nodded at the priest, stepped lightly down the outside stairs, and walked a couple of blocks. Still feeling empty, I knelt down on the sidewalk and completed the last couple of prayers of my rosary. A woman gazed at me from behind the limp pink curtains of her living room window. Maybe she thought I was crazy like Mom. Maybe I was. I didn't care. I just wanted to feel full again.

A few days later, I claimed the 8 x 10 picture of Christ that Dad had brought home from Grandma's. To make room, I unplugged the record player from the table next to my bed and tried to sneak it into the garage. Dad caught me as I went past him with it in the living room. "How would you like it if I shoved all *my* garbage into your closet?" he fumed. Dad was building cabinets for his tools in the garage. The cabinets wouldn't be perfect, but he would save money by doing it himself. So he was particular about the garage and kept it neat. When I apologized, he shrugged and made a place for it.

I placed the framed picture on the table. Like headshots of celebrities, the depiction was Christ in all his glory: young and handsome with flowing hair and large, watery eyes. His right hand pointed upward toward his Father. His heart was aflame in his chest. Thinking back, I can almost see Christ's signature etched across the bottom ("Love ya always, Christ, your Lord").

Each night after I closed my door, I knelt next to my bed as I had when I was young, and I prayed.

After Sue moved to Los Altos for school, Joan rearranged the upstairs bedroom they had shared. She moved her bed into Sue's old spot next to the stereo and brought in a striped deck chair she'd bought. When she dumped Sue's mattress in my room, I complained. But Joan, like Mom, could put a spin on things that made it seem like she was doing you a favor: "This way, Peg, your friends will have someplace to sleep when they come over."

When Sue came home that spring of 1969 she was relaxed, bordering on spunky. She held her chin higher than she did before she left home, her eyes more wide open as though breathless with all they were seeing away from home for the first time. Though she was disturbed by Joan's power play of removing her bed from the upstairs bedroom, she refused to lose her cool. Her clenched teeth behind her smile, however, were a dead giveaway. "I've been erased," she said at dinner. She was laughing, but her bottom teeth pushed against her top teeth, which was a sign that she was irritated.

Joan was unapologetic. She needed more space, and that was that.

So Sue moved in with me, which irked me—I now liked being alone in my room. Sue was stretching on the bedroom floor the first night when I came in, her long hair covering her face as she laid her head on her knees, her hands holding her feet. Though majoring in English literature, she was taking a dance class and seemed to stretch all the time. Soon she was done, and she climbed into the sleeping bag on her mattress.

"I see you got Grandma's picture." Sue said, pointing her chin at the Christ on the table. Sue hadn't been to church since Midnight Mass on Christmas Eve the year before. I nodded, hoping she would drop it. I was tempted to skip my prayers that night, but Christ's eyes bored into me. Was my faith so weak that I couldn't stand a little embarrassment? I turned off the bedroom light and knelt down next to my bed, acutely conscious of Sue's eyes on me. I bowed my head, made the sign of the cross, and put my hands together. For a second, I imagined Sue getting off her mattress and kneeling next to me, saying prayers together as we had in church for so many years. The thought made me cringe. Maybe she would at least have the manners not to take any notice.

But Sue's voice rose out of the darkness. "I know you're happy I'm back, Peg, but you don't need to bow down to me."

Her sense of humor had returned, although not at the most convenient time for me. "Shut up," I said.

Maybe she had lost her faith, but I still had mine.

Mom, on the other hand, had stopped going to church altogether. She said she thought the church was too hypocritical. I didn't want to hear why. Sunday Mass was comforting to me. Sermon followed song followed prayer in the same order every week. You knew what to expect.

Chapter 10

☞❦☜

Miss Scarlet and the Whos

April, 1969

Joan threw the blurry Polaroid photo on the floor. I picked it up. I could make out a shirtless Dan surrounded by giggling naked Asian girls.

"He thinks it's cute." Joan grabbed the photo from me and ripped it to pieces. She blew her nose. "I'm sick of living my life around his stupid letters!" (I noticed though, to my disappointment, that she scooped the pieces of the photograph up again and stuffed them in an envelope.)

Hoping to change the subject, I put Joan's Aretha Franklin album on the stereo. I knew I made a mistake when I heard the first chords: "The moment I wake up, before I put on my makeup, I say a little prayer for you ..." Joan had sung the tune countless times, no doubt thinking of Danny. Now she closed her eyes.

"Don't ever fall so much in love with someone that what they want determines what you want."

"What do you mean?" I asked.

Joan said nothing.

* * *

Glenn, still at SF State, worked as a bartender in the City, driving around in "Miss Scarlet," his red Volkswagen convertible. When he moved to an apartment in North Beach, he had to leave Scarlet in our garage—even in those days, parking a pint-size VW in North Beach was impossible—where she languished for weeks without being driven until the day Joan received a postcard with a picture of North Beach from him that read: "Miss Scarlet needs you to drive her or her battery will die. Love, Grinch."

Glenn had become the grinch after we all watched *How the Grinch Stole Christmas*, the light from the small screen casting a greenish glow upon him. "Please call me Grinch. I like to grinch things the way the Grinch grinched presents from the little Who people (It was true—we had all experienced a Grinch moment—an album pinched, a beloved book gone; after one of Glenn's visits, Patrick would barely have any clothes left to wear). Then, when I'm feeling generous, I sometimes ..." giving Patrick a sideways glance and a wily smile, "give them back."

Joan mashed the clutch, threw the car in reverse, and peeled out of our quiet side street like Andretti out of the pit. The top down, I held my hair down with one hand and reached for the radio knob with the other.

"Broken," Joan said matter-of-factly. The Grinch didn't have the money to fix it. He was saving his money to go to Europe. He must have really wanted to go: Glenn not having a radio was like the pope not having a rosary.

Joan's chin tipped up as we drove, her eyes ahead of the curves. Feet warmed by the heater, hair whipping our cold faces, we *vroomed* along the twisting roads of Tilden Park, shooting through thick pockets of fog caught in the thick brush and redwoods, until we reached the top. Joan pulled into a turnout. In the distance, San Francisco glimmered like the Emerald City. I couldn't wait for the day I could call it my own.

After winding our way back down, we arrived at Jerry's Beefburgers, a hangout for the high school crowd. Joan walked up to the window to order. I stayed in the car. Somebody whistled, and Joan's face reddened. When she came back to the car, she handed off her Diet Coke and fries without even looking at me. Joan looked through the steering wheel surreptitiously, a hunter spying on its prey. "Who are you looking at?" I whispered.

"An adorable guy named Larry from my history class. Oh, God, he's coming over. Eat my fries and act normal."

A movie star with long, dark hair had materialized next to Joan's door. I crammed a handful of fries into my mouth to explain my inability to speak.

"What a great car! Mind if I get in?" Joan nodded, radiant.

Before long, Joan and Larry became a couple. The Grinch's hot set of wheels had landed the little Who a boyfriend. Mom, who had always been fond of Dan, liked Larry too. "If you love 'em, I love 'em," seemed to be Mom's philosophy with all of our relationships. That was fine, but where I was concerned, she only had to love Paul. We were going to be together forever.

* * *

In May, Dad and his siblings received a small inheritance from Grandma and Grandpa's estate. Uncle Jim would stay in Grandma and Grandpa's house. With the money, Mom and Dad bought a dining room set and hutch, new carpeting, and airline tickets to Europe for Glenn and Pat.

"You can use all that money you've saved for food and places to stay, Grinchie," Mom said proudly into the phone one night.

"But you're going to have to take that brother of yours with you."
She laughed, knowing Glenn would be thrilled to travel with
Patrick. Mom had booked my brothers' flights for mid-June: a
few weeks after the end of their college semesters and a few days
after I graduated from junior high school.

*   *   *

June, 1969

Groups of emancipated shoulder-slumped girls with tall hair
and gangs of boys with untucked shirts and shoes too big for their
skinny legs burst through the double doors of Bancroft Junior
High, anticipating three glorious months of summer vacation.
I waited for Paul outside the doors where we always met after
school, but he didn't come. My friend Bonnie waited with me.

"Come on, Peg, let's just go. He's probably hanging out with
his friends. It *is* the last day of school," she tugged on my blouse.

No one else was coming out. Paul had been acting strangely
lately, cutting our conversations short and staying after school to
play football instead of walking home with me.

"You're right, let's go," I sighed, sad that I wouldn't be able to
celebrate with Paul on the last day of ninth grade.

Footsteps of someone running. Paul? It was, with a group
of other kids, but his expression was distant. "Hi," he said to
me. He scratched his hand nervously while some of his friends
walking with girls behind us pushed each other playfully.

"Hi."

Paul shifted his feet. "Um … I don't know how to say this …
Next year, we'll be in high school, and I want to have a fresh start."

I nodded. I guessed what he meant, but I didn't want it to
be true. My heart hammered in my chest. Bonnie looked away,
embarrassed. I was silent. No use making it easy for him.

He looked at the sidewalk. "I think we should break up for a while."

I opened my mouth, but no words came out. I nodded. We both just stood there wordlessly.

He shifted his feet again, and ran a hand through his hair. "Okay, well, maybe I'll call you sometime during the summer." He walked back to his friends.

A minute later I heard his laugh ring through a babble of conversation. I had known that laugh on my front porch and on sidewalks, on buses and in my thoughts as I lay with my head on my pillow each night for the past two years. Paul's laugh had always belonged to me. Now it sounded different, as though he was laughing in a foreign language.

I hurried away, toward my house. Bonnie ran to keep up. I used my sleeve to wipe my nose.

We were quiet as we walked home. When we reached my porch she said, "He's an asshole, Peg. You want me to stay?"

"No thanks. I'll be okay." I climbed the stairs to the front door.

"Peg, is that you?" Mom called from her room as I came in. She had taken a part-time job as a maid at a hotel near the Oakland airport. Although it was not exactly the type of moving-up-in-the-world sort of job that she would have liked, it helped to pay the bills. Both Paul and Bonnie's families employed maids, and now my mother had become one. I added her job to my list of secrets. "How was your last day of school, honey?" Mom called cheerfully.

"Not great." I stopped at her bedroom door. I choked out the words, "Paul broke up with me."

"Oh, honey …" she said, getting up to comfort me like when I'd fallen down and skinned a knee.

I put my hand up to stop her. Her pity would have only made me feel worse: I was fourteen, for God's sakes. "I'm okay, Mom." I dizzily walked into my bedroom. I locked my door, walked over to my mattress, and lay down, burying my face deep into my pillow. *One one thousand, two one thousand,* if I held my breath long enough, maybe I would suffocate. *Thirty one thousand, thirty-one one thousand... .*

Outside the darkness there was knocking.

"Peg?" Joan's voice was far away. "PEG?" The knocking grew insistent. Mumbling outside my door ... I looked around ... it was still light outside ... Joan and Mom's voices.

I stumbled to the door.

Mom frowned. "Egetha, we were worried about you."

"I'm fine," I sniffed, wiping my face with my hands before climbing back into bed.

Joan sat down on my mattress. Never comfortable with affection, she fluffed my hair with her hand.

"So you and Paul broke up?" she asked.

I nodded at the wall.

"You know, Peg, you can hang out with me and my friends next year." She and Larry had broken up, too, and her circle of friends had widened.

The thought of school made me realize that from now on I would see Paul in the corridors, and we would just pass each other by. I wrapped my arms around my stomach and rocked.

"My friends and I will be seniors, and Paul and all his friends will be lowly sophomores."

I stopped rocking as Joan's words seeped in. I smiled.

Joan's laugh trilled like a bird's on a sunny spring morning.

I wiped the tears from my eyes. If Paul and I had to break up, this was definitely the year to do it.

* * *

Glenn and Pat came home to stay with us the night before they left for Europe. "I'm up for a little folly on the continent, aren't you?" Glenn warbled to Pat at the dinner table, a line from the high school musical in which the two of them had starred as

British jewel thieves. I was still sullen after the break up with Paul, and their giddiness irritated me. Not Mom and Dad though; they were giddy too, laughing hard, and wanting, I think, to feel a part of my brothers' upcoming odyssey.

"Why can't *we* go to Europe, Mom?" Joan sulked, pushing a pea around her plate.

"Because the boys are older, and they want to go more." Joan rolled her eyes. I tucked Mom's answer away for future reference, taking my place in the buffet line behind my brothers. One day, I'd go to Europe, too. I just had to really want it.

Glenn and Pat skipped from country to country, staying in youth hostels and with friends they made along the way. Postcards from Paris, London, and Rome arrived, Glenn gushing about the architecture and Patrick cramming in hilarious stories. Glenn fell in love with a young Italian man (that part didn't make it into the postcard: Mom and Dad still hoped that Glenn would find the proverbial "nice girl"), who invited them to stay at his family's home in a village in Tuscany. Pat's postcard went on about homemade pasta and Chianti, and laughing into the wee hours of the night with their new friend's family. At the bottom he added, almost as an afterthought: "Glenn's been in the hospital with a bad case of asthma."

A week after Pat's postcard arrived, we received another one from Glenn. It read simply, "Patrick is a Pig."

Pat got home in early September so that he could return to UC Santa Cruz, while Glenn traveled on to Nice, where he stayed for another month, making money pulling barnacles from boats. Sometime during his stay there, I received a letter spewing romantic French poetry from a certain Jean-Claude who had supposedly fallen head over heels in love with me after Glenn showed him my picture. True or not, the letter worked wonders for my wounded self-esteem. Even from afar the Grinch was looking out for me.

Chapter 11

❧

The Never Ending Loop

October, 1969

"Hey, Joan, nice skirt," Joan's friend Theresa said as she passed me digging in my locker. Theresa was the senior class secretary, and Joan had recently been elected class president. I wore the rust-colored ankle-length skirt that I'd given Joan for Christmas the previous year. Over the summer, at Joan's urging, I had eaten more than just Grape Nuts, apples and licorice, and my figure had filled out enough to fit in Joan's clothes. Our hair was identical: straight, blonde, a few inches past our shoulders. People said we looked alike. I was flattered; Joan quietly put up with it.

Theresa stared straight at me. "So, Joan, where did you get the skirt?" I waited, but when she didn't catch on, I didn't want to embarrass her.

"Um, I picked it up at the Goodwill," I said into my armful of books, sure that she'd realize I wasn't Joan when I spoke.

"I love it! I'll have to go back there. I never seem to find cool things when I go. See you at the meeting this afternoon."

I screamed into my hand.

Our family had always been close, due in part to my mother's illness. Now, as Glenn, Pat, and Sue ventured out on their own, I'd stuck close to Joan.

One morning during a break at school I was buying a candy bar when I heard a familiar voice behind me. "Don't get that one. There were moths in the last one I bought." It was Paul. He leaned against the vending machine as my PayDay clunked into the tray. My face got warmer.

"You're lying," I said.

"I swear. Not just moths, but *hundreds* of moth eggs."

I'd forgotten how handsome he was: bright blue eyes beneath long curled eyelashes, perfectly shaped nose, and oh God, those curls at the nape of his neck. The smell of English Leather was intoxicating. I stepped back. "I don't believe you," I said, crossing my arms and raising my eyebrows.

The bell rang. "Suit yourself," he said. He waved and walked away.

My fluttering heart transported me to Mrs. Dickie's English class.

Vera Dickie was small and perky with black pointed glasses. She'd taught most of my siblings and didn't hide the fact that I was her pet. During study time, she called me up to her desk. My eyes were drawn to the black bracelet she wore on her wrist.

"I have to say I'm sorry that you're the last Kennedy I'll be teaching, Peg," she said softly. "Couldn't your mother have had more children?" She laughed, and a few curious students looked in our direction. Oh, what little she knew. "You know that it will probably be up to you to continue those marvelous Kennedy genes, don't you?"

"Why?" I asked.

"Well, Glenn's the scholar, and Pat's a great showman and artist; your sister Sue's the rebel, but a poet. I had her in my poetry class a few years ago, and she was really quite talented. Joan I don't know as well. But somehow, I feel it in my bones: continuing those Kennedy genes will be up to you."

* * *

November, 1969

Dad, Joan, Mom, and I were eating dinner one evening in early November when the phone rang. Joan answered, "Just a minute," her voice high pitched and anxious as she quickly handed the phone to Mom. Something was wrong. Dad's fork hung suspended in midair as he watched Mom.

"Yes, officer." Mom straightened her posture as she always did when talking with authority figures, a throwback to her institutional stays. She grabbed a pen off the counter and swung her hand around as she looked for something to write on. Joan ripped out the back page from the leather-bound phone book. God only knows what was already written on it. "Santa Cruz General, thank you so much, officer," Mom said.

Oh my God, it's Pat. My heart was exploding.

Mom handed Joan the phone then covered her face with her hands as she composed herself. My hands clasped together as I silently prayed he was alright.

"Patrick's been in an accident." She took a deep breath. "Joanie, get me Glenn's new number," she said as she picked up the phone and quickly dialed a number from memory. Mom rallied for emergencies. "I hope Susie's at home," she said under her breath.

"Daddy, go get the car keys," she said as she waited for Sue to pick up. "We need to get down to Santa Cruz."

"Susie, honey, Patrick's been in a car accident. I don't know—I got a call from the police department. Meet us at Santa Cruz General." Mom enunciated every syllable when she was nervous; chaos seemed to calm her down. Suddenly, I felt a pang of jealousy. From Los Altos, Sue would get to Patrick before we would.

Mom called Glenn and told him to meet us at the hospital, too. When she hung up the phone, she grabbed her purse, and we all ran to the car.

No one spoke. It was understood that Patrick was still alive. Why else would Mom let Dad drive at breakneck speed to the freeway? I was angry at the familiar San Leandro streets. Were so many stoplights necessary in the deserted night streets? Normally, Dad wouldn't even run a yellow light. That evening we sped through the red ones.

* * *

The car landed upside down on top of a lone tree growing out of a cliff, fifty feet beneath the Highway 1, and fifty feet above the ocean below it, "caught," as Mom would say, "by the hand of God." Just a couple of weeks before, Mom had bought Pat a new battery for the car which kept its lone headlight shining. Without it, no one would have known they were there.

Pat and his friends hung upside down for more than an hour. Patrick, his pelvic bone crushed by the steering wheel, was conscious, as were two of his other passengers, who were also badly injured. They cried out, terrified at the sight of the crashing waves and large craggy rocks fifty feet below. By the time the police cars, ambulance, and truck with crane came, Patrick told us later, everything had gone black. He didn't remember being reeled up, or arriving at the hospital.

At the hospital, Mom and Dad were the only ones allowed to go in to see Pat in the intensive care unit. Glenn, Sue, Joan, and I rushed up to them when they emerged.

"Well, the poor baby looks terrible, but the doctor told us that he's going to be okay." Mom said, dabbing her eyes with a tissue. Dad was unable to speak, his clenched jaw a dam against a torrent of tears.

We drove around downtown Santa Cruz until we found a motel with a vacancy. Mom and Dad could afford two rooms for two nights: one room for them and one for Glenn, Sue, Joan, and me. After that, Mom would stay to visit Pat while we would leave to go back to school and work.

At night, we siblings mixed the pouches of Sanka provided near the bathroom sink with hot tap water and drank it to stay awake, playing Hearts until we couldn't keep our eyes open. Glenn slept on the floor, while we girls shared the king-sized bed.

During the day, we hung out at the hospital while Mom and Dad took turns in the room with Pat. When the rest of us returned home, Mom stayed at the motel, calling us with updates.

By Thanksgiving a couple of weeks later, Pat was doing a little better. His friend Mary offered our family the place she and Pat rented with a few other students. The house was close to the hospital, and all of them were going home for Thanksgiving break.

A faded red bicycle with thick tires leaned against the porch railing of the yellow Victorian house shared by Pat and his roommates. Next to the bike was a grooved brass lamp with faded silk shade. Traffic's "Dear Mr. Fantasy" blared out the screen door. Dad rang the doorbell several times before Mary hurried to the door. Mary had narrow brown eyes, thin lips, and thick brown hair that she flipped behind her shoulder with a quick impatient motion of her hand.

"Patrick will be so glad that you're all here," she said as she ushered us into the living room, "He always talks about you. Oh my God, I wasn't prepared to have so much enamel in my house—you all have such huge teeth!" On cue, all six of us gave her a toothy smile. Her giggle was an unexpectedly deep chirrup which made us laugh again. No wonder Patrick liked her.

The wooden floor was slivering from heavy traffic near the front door. Handmade afghan blankets covered threadbare couches and chairs. Vintage hats with feathers hung like wilting flowers from a rack standing by the couch. A rusted watering can sat on the floor next to a large fern on a stand. We set our suitcases on the living room floor. Books were jammed in a case behind the couch next to a crate full of albums. I ruffled through them. *Hmmm ... Joni Mitchell, Judy Collins ... Beatles White Album ... I could get comfortable in this house.*

Just as I kneeled down to make a more thorough inspection, Dad said, "Okay, sports, time to go."

We crammed into the Plymouth Duster and headed to the hospital.

Once she was through the double doors, Mom's heels went into locomotive mode, powering her across the linoleum to the elevators. The rest of us ran to catch up. "Pat's still in intensive care—thank God we have insurance," Mom said. I understand her relief now: Daddy's health insurance covered almost all of Pat's hospital expenses. Without it, we'd have had to sell our house.

Mom and Dad went in first to see Pat. They emerged smiling. "He's sitting up. He looks much better," Mom said. Daddy's jaw relaxed.

I was surprised to hear laughter when Glenn went in. The head nurse pushed open the door and leaned in admonishing, "If he laughs too hard he'll rip his stitches." Although the laughter grew quieter behind the closed door, it didn't stop.

Glenn returned to the waiting room and sat next to me on the armless sofa. When I asked what he and Pat had been laughing about, he said he'd reminded Pat of how miserable he'd been, suffering from asthma in the little hospital in Italy, while Pat had been pampered with wine, pasta, and tiramisu. And how, when Patrick finally had found leisure to come to the hospital, he'd sat sweating like a stuffed pig at the end of Glenn's hospital bed. "He couldn't even converse, the pig," Glenn said, indignant again at the memory. But when he took a magazine from the coffee table, he didn't look at it. Instead, he pulled out a handkerchief and held it over his eyes for a good long minute.

I stood in line behind Joan in the corridor by Pat's room. Sue took a deep breath and pushed open the door, which closed behind her. Soon Sue was chatting away, as though she and Pat were talking about the latest issue of *Art Forum* magazine. We wondered what she could be saying. We couldn't hear Pat. She came out with shoulders slumped. "He slept the whole time," she said. She stalked over to the nurse who sat behind the reception desk reading a paperback book.

"Excuse me," Sue, at nineteen already our family's spokesperson on all things medical, said curtly, "We'd like to talk with my brother's doctor."

The nurse looked up. "I'm sorry, but he's only here on Tuesdays and Thursdays. He'll be by tomorrow." The woman went back to her book.

Sue handed her a long list of questions. "Could you please make sure that the doctor receives this?"

The nurse smiled wryly and nodded.

Joan's shrill laugh came through the door, along with what sounded like a response from Patrick. *Okay, as soon as she comes out, I'm going in before he falls asleep again.* A few minutes later, I grabbed the door from Joan as she came out. A figure on the bed waved me to come toward him. *Good God, that can't be Patrick!* A bandage covered the whole top of his head down to his eyebrows. His eyes were sunken, his face, deeply bruised. A cast enveloped his torso, which lay immobile against the slightly inclined bed. Tubes ran up his nose and IVs protruded from both arms. I moved next to the bed and patted his hand carefully. He took my hand and smiled, his eyelids fighting to stay open. I searched my brain for something to say. "I got the Beatles' *White Album.* My favorite song is 'Blackbird,' but I also like 'Julia,' and 'I Will' ..." *God, I'm rambling.* He smiled and raised his eyebrows to show that I'd already told him, and he thought it was great. *Of course I'd told him. We'd talked about it a couple of months ago. What a ninny I am! What if this is the last time I ever talk to him? He'll die thinking I'm a ninny.*

Pat was losing the battle with his eyelids. When they finally closed, he didn't even try to open them.

"Okay, visiting hours are over, sweetheart," the nurse said, entering the room. Patrick squeezed my hand weakly. I walked toward the door. When I turned to look one more time, the curtain around him had already been closed.

* * *

Early December, 1969

I wasn't sick, not really. The wind had kept me awake the night before whipping the bushes against my bedroom window. My body was fine but my spirit was in turmoil, and the thought of getting dressed and going to school was overwhelming. Mom allowed me to stay home.

I got up and wandered the house. Mom and Dad were both at work and Joan was at school. With no one there, the house was just a collection of lifeless furniture. I wasn't sure what I was looking for. I walked through the den into the living room and sat for a minute, feet tucked beneath me, on the green tweed chair. I gazed above the fireplace at the canvas Pat painted the year before while studying Northern Renaissance art. A young woman in a headscarf, peasant top and skirt sat barefoot, hand on chin. Her expression was rapturous. She seemed to be looking at something extraordinary, but what? What was it about the painting that comforted me? Was it because Patrick had painted it? Maybe so, but his other paintings in the house didn't have the same allure.

The detail on the woman's clothing was so delicately rendered that I could almost feel the smoothness of silk and velvet. I touched the rough painted texture. How could it look so soft and feel so coarse? The disparity made me sad and confused. Was I going crazy like Mom? I wanted to step into that picture and feel the rapture she was feeling. Life was nothing but a series of sad events. Good things never lasted. I wanted to go somewhere where there was no sorrow, and I wouldn't feel any pain.

I walked up the stairs to Joan's bed and buried myself beneath her heavy blankets. I wedged my face deep into her pillow, which smelled of Vicks Vaporub (Joan, who was just getting over a cold, swore by the stuff) and slipped into darkness.

It was odd to wake up in the late morning of a school day and hear Maude and Andy, our elderly neighbors across the street, talking to the mailman. I imagined them afterward struggling, as they always did, to get themselves into the car.

I had never seen this room from this angle, lying down. It looked longer than I remembered it. To my surprise, without any of my siblings there, it was only a room.

I turned to the right and saw the tiny clusters of Sue's handwriting on the wall. Luckily, Joan still hadn't seen fit to paint the walls. I crawled to the end of the bed and leaned in so I could see. *It's funny I never thought to read them before.* I read the quotes as Sue had apparently written them, in columns from left to right.

Yes, Father! Yes, and always yes! —St. Francis de Sales

The world there is full,
The world here is full.
Fullness from fullness proceeds.
After taking fully from the full,
It still remains completely full.
—Upanishads, Chapter 5

If you cannot find the truth right where you are, where else do you expect to find it? —Dogen

The aim of life is to live, and to live means to be aware, joyously, drunkenly, serenely, divinely aware.
—Henry Miller

It loved to happen.
—Marcus Aurelius

"Seymour told me 'Shine your shoes for the Fat Lady'... Are you listening to me? There isn't anyone out there who isn't Seymour's Fat Lady... And don't you know – don't you know who that Fat Lady really is? Ah, buddy. Ah, buddy. It's Christ Himself. Christ, Himself, buddy."
—J.D. Salinger, Franny and Zooey

I gasped. This, finally, was something I understood. The Fat Lady was Mom and Dad, and all my brothers and sisters. The Fat Lady was me and Paul and everyone I'd ever liked or not liked. Life had a purpose after all, and the purpose was *to be*. And the only way to understand that—to understand that while living—was through treating others with love and compassion.

I felt my heart expand in my chest. The very colors of the house seemed brighter.

I trotted down the stairs to Mom and Dad's room, opened Mom's bill drawer, and took out a piece of paper and an envelope. On the paper I wrote, "I finally understand the wall." I folded the paper, addressed the envelope, affixed a stamp, threw a robe over my nightgown, and ran out to the sidewalk. I cupped my ear: the mail truck was down the block. Running as fast as my legs could carry me, I caught up with it just before Bonnie's house.

I was breathless as I handed the mailman my envelope. He glanced at my robe and bare feet warily as he slipped it in his bag.

"Go back inside, little lady. You'll catch your death out here like that," he said shaking his head.

A couple of weeks later, I got a letter back. I walked to my bedroom, sat down on the bed, and carefully opened the envelope, unfolding its contents with anticipation.

"Dear Peg: I can't tell you how happy your letter made me. You're the only one that ever acknowledged the wall." Underneath a drawing of a potato surrounded by a glowing halo was written: *"Celebrate ... Eat a Potato. Love, Sue."*

Chapter 12

꙰

Patrick

Mid-December, 1969

Patrick was coming home. All morning I waited. Finally, the car drove up and Glenn and Dad helped Patrick out of the Duster and into his wheelchair in front of our house. His lips curled in pain as they moved him. His shoulders sagged, his arms dropped loosely by his sides. His cheekbones looked sunken beneath the bandage wrapped round his head; his corduroy bell-bottoms, once snug, now swam on his motionless legs. I ran down the stairs and opened the front door.

The corners of Pat's mouth turned up when he saw me. I caught my breath quietly so he wouldn't know what a shock it was to have my eyes meet his in a wheelchair. He was so thin! The bandage wrapped round his head squished his eyebrows down so that he wore a constant frown. His hazel eyes, surrounded by dark circles, were cloudy. I moved aside, opening the door wider to allow Glenn and Dad to lift his wheelchair from the front porch into the foyer, turning my head so Pat couldn't see my tears.

Mom entered from the kitchen. Seeming to ignore the wheelchair, Pat's useless legs, and the huge white bandage on his head, she took Pat's hand. "Hurrah—Atarick's home!"

Pat's near loss had made him the furnace that our family warmed itself at. Footsteps came down the stairs, and soon Sue and Joan had joined the rest of us in the foyer. Pat rubbed his eyes wearily. "I just want to take a nap," he said, his lips tightening into a rueful smile.

Glenn collapsed the sides of Pat's wheelchair so that it could get through the door of the den. Dad and Glenn lifted Pat onto the bed that had been borrowed from Aunt Noreen. The two maple couches had been squeezed into the garage next to Glenn's car. Dad hadn't complained one bit about crowding his space.

* * *

Pajama-clad on Christmas morning, I sat in the green tweed chair reading the comics. Joan was on the couch, legs tucked under her robe as she read the style section of the paper. Sue sat upright on the floor in leotard and leg warmers, legs straight as her arms grasped the arches of her feet: a stretching exercise I'd seen her do a million times since she'd come home for the holidays.

Dad knelt by the fireplace and struck a match under the kindling he'd carefully arranged above a couple of bigger logs. From the hall, there was a scrape against the bathroom door jam and a loud "Dammit!" Patrick's frustration grew with each passing day.

Dad turned expectantly in that direction. I looked down, wanting to delay the sight of Pat in a wheelchair for a few more seconds. "Well, there he is!" Dad said, grinning as Pat's wheels rolled toward us across the carpet.

On cue, we all looked up and smiled. I searched Pat's face. Was he sad, as he had been last night, or bitter, as he'd been yesterday? Should I offer to get him anything? No, it might make him feel more helpless. I turned back to the comics again, hoping to display normalcy as I watched him from the corner of my eye.

Pat adjusted himself in his chair and grimaced. He took his pain medication with meals and hadn't eaten yet. To make matters worse, the night before, he'd received a call from his friend Michael, a passenger in the car accident, who informed Pat that Debra, another friend and passenger still in a coma, might have permanent brain damage.

Mom came in from the kitchen in red robe and slippers. "Pat, honey, can I get you some coffee?" she asked. Pat nodded. His eyes followed her back through the kitchen door, his listless gaze fixed on the door long after she had passed through it. He closed his eyes for a few seconds and sighed. Had I been the one in the wheelchair, Pat would have taken my hand. "Don't worry, Peggle," he'd have said, "pretty soon you'll feel much better and be able to do things for yourself." But I was the little sister, and my saying those things to Pat would have only reminded him that he was incapable of walking into the kitchen to get his own coffee.

Mom brought Pat a tray with coffee, toast, and medication and set it down on his lap. Pat sucked in his upper lip and stared at the tray. "Thanks, Mom," His voice was barely audible.

Glenn, usually able to lighten Pat's mood, sailed in and sat down next to Pat's wheelchair. He must have seen our pleading looks. *Say something, Glenn. Make him feel better.*

Glenn didn't let us down. Up until then, Glenn carefully avoided sounding faggish in front of my parents, but Pat's dark mood called for drastic measures. "So did we have a nice nap, Princess Poopoo?" he asked, grabbing Pat's hand.

Dad shook his head and frowned at Glenn's girlish tone.

Pat cracked a small smile. He shook his head and closed his eyes as if to warn Glenn he was in no mood to laugh, but Glenn continued.

"Is the Princess Poopoo ready to open presents?" Glenn asked, his voice now morphing into the Grinch. Patrick shoulders shook as he giggled. Glenn's Grinch always made him laugh.

Daddy's frown disappeared as it seemed to dawn on him what Glenn was trying to do.

"… because if the Princess Poopoo doesn't open her presents, the Grinch will have to open them and keep them." Glenn smiled a wily Grinch smile as he drummed his long fingers together greedily.

Patrick bent over in laughter.

"Okay, okay, I'll open my presents," Patrick said a minute later, wiping his eyes with the napkin Mom had brought with his coffee.

Dad scooted over next to the tree, picked up a present, and read the gift tag. Earlier I'd anticipated with great pleasure the gifts I might receive. But Glenn had given us the best gift: Patrick's spirit, returned.

*　*　*

The better mood did not last. The day after Christmas, the curtains in the den were drawn. I squinted to see better in the darkness. Pat leaned against his pillows, eyes fixed on the covered window. When his pelvis had slammed against the steering wheel, the balls of his hips had come out of their sockets and been crushed. The doctors said he would probably never walk again. "Can I open the curtains for you? I asked.

"No," he replied glumly. "Keep them closed."

The next day, Pat did not get out of bed. The one day turned into two, then three. On the fourth day, even Glenn, who was usually able to convince Pat to do things, emerged from Pat's room, head down.

At dinner that night, Pat rolled into what had become his place at the head of the table. The large bandage on his head was yellowed, his hair, matted, from lying in bed for so long. His expression was dour. But he had ventured out.

"Pat, I can't say that I've *ever* seen you looking better!" Glenn said.

We held our breath. This time Glenn had gone too far!

Pat's eyes were dull. "Do you guys know how *shitty* I feel? I honestly don't know what to do."

Mom took Pat's hand. "Do what makes you happy. Draw … paint. We'll get you everything you need, Atarick."

"I don't know if I can, Mom," Pat said as he pushed the bandage up off his nose where a sore had formed, "I don't feel like doing anything."

"I know, honey," Mom replied, taking his hand. "Just try."

Pat slapped the wheelchair with his other hand. "I don't think it'll do any good."

Mom clutched his hand tighter. "Just make a list."

The next morning, Joan and I came back from the art store with oil paints, brushes, pencils, drawing pads, and stretched canvases.

As we unloaded the supplies in the den, Pat asked, "Can you guys bring that upstairs? I want to work there."

Dad was at the firehouse and Glenn at his apartment. Sue had driven back to school that morning with a friend.

"Well, honey," Mom hesitated, "I … I don't think the girls and I can carry you upstairs."

"I know, Mom," Pat replied with a hint of a smile. "I'll figure it out."

Later that afternoon, I heard a scratching sound in the stairwell. I leaned out my door to see Patrick on the third stair, hands wrapped around the banister as around a rope in mountain climbing.

"Hey, Peggle," he said with the mischievous grin that I'd thought was gone for good.

"You need some help?" I asked.

"Nope, I'm fine," he said taking a breath before hoisting himself up to the next step. "Could you bring me a cup of coffee?"

I filled the coffeepot with water, measured coffee, and plugged the pot in. The fragrant aroma filled the air, the smell of a fresh day full of possibilities.

"How did you get up here?" Joan asked from her bedroom upstairs, her voice rising to a giggle.

The next morning, a new routine set in. By the time the rest of us left the house, Patrick would be upstairs. At the end of the day, he would show us his work. Some days he seemed to get stuck and would draw the same image over and over again. Other days, we'd come home to find the room overflowing with sketches.

"Peg, listen to this," Pat said to me one afternoon while placing the needle on an album.

I lay on the floor eyes closed and breathed in deep, pleased that he wanted to explore songs with me again.

"Buffalo Springfield ... definitely the best song on the album," he said. I nodded enthusiastically.

He handed me a pencil and sketchpad. "Draw me a picture, Peg."

I drew, as always, copying the way Patrick held his pencil, shading, dark next to the line, then lighter, gradually fading away, until I'd completed drawing a fold of fabric similar to the one Patrick had drawn that morning. I proudly handed it to him.

"That's nice. Now draw me a picture that's yours alone."

Confused—I had drawn the picture, so, it was, therefore, mine. I took the pad and started over. As I drew, Indians on a plain, rocks and brush took shape. When I was done, I held it up. The figures weren't lifelike, but that was okay. They were mine.

Pat scooted across the floor. "I love it!" he exclaimed. "Nice landscape—great expressions!" He took my hand. "Find your own style if you want to create something memorable."

Chapter 13

❦

The Giant Dipper

For four months, Pat's visits to the doctor yielded no encouraging news, but Pat kept exercising in his warm baths. That April, the doctor noted that Pat's hips seemed to have more flexibility. He asked Pat to return in May for tests. To the doctor's amazement those tests revealed that fluid had returned to Pat's hip sockets. Pat was given a pair of crutches and was told to start walking.

That evening was filled with joyously tearful phone calls from Mom to Sue and Glenn and all of our aunts and uncles. Daddy's face took on a rested look that I hadn't seen in ages as he watched Pat hobble through the living room and down the hallway, his leg movements becoming smoother as his muscles remembered their purpose. When I opened my bedroom door that night, Patrick entered more like Gene Kelly than a guy who had just gotten out of a wheelchair, grinning broadly as he stood one crutch still while he hobbled round it in a circle. Back on his feet, Patrick was once again our showman.

Just as quickly as he came home, Pat wasted no time leaving. After two weeks on crutches, he made arrangements to move back in with his old roommates in Santa Cruz. The following Saturday, while Dad was at work and Joan was overseeing a Senior Class car wash, Pat's friend Richard came by. My stomach tightened at the knock on the door.

Before I could get up, Pat was lippity-lopping on his crutches through the dining room toward the front door. Mom and I followed. Ever since Pat had come home broken and frail six months before, his pulse had become ours. Now that he was healed, his heart was his alone. It was time for him to go. Richard picked up Pat's duffle bag in the foyer and carried it out to his car.

Pat leaned forward and gave Mom a hug. He then turned to me.

"I left something on your bed," he said, hugging me.

The wooden artist's box, filled with all the supplies that Joan and I bought for Pat just months before, lay on my Indian bedspread. On top was a note in Patrick's handwriting, "Create something memorable, Peg."

* * *

June, 1970

When Joan threw her cap up in the air after her graduation ceremony, some of her hair, which was crimped and full of electricity, stood on end. From where I sat in the front row with my family, Joan looked like a lioness ready to pounce on the world. I was grateful that she'd decided to go to UC Berkeley and live her first year at home.

Soon after her graduation, Joan received a letter from Danny, her first in over a year. She ran upstairs to read it. A few minutes later, she stuck her head in my bedroom doorway and beamed.

"Danny's been discharged!" she blurted out.

"Why?" I asked, bewildered. He wasn't supposed to be out of the navy for at least another year.

She threw up her hands and shook her head, grinning dazedly. "He got caught with some pot. They wanted to court-martial him; but he'd been selling weed to some of his superiors, and they didn't want that to get out. He got an honorable discharge! He's coming home next week."

She seemed awfully excited for someone who'd said "good riddance" only one year earlier.

* * *

"Hey, Pegs!" Sue, barefoot in sleeveless leotard and leggings, hair cropped short, said breathlessly as I entered the living room. African drums pounded from the small turntable on the floor. Sue had graduated from Foothill Junior College down in Los Altos and was home for the summer. Her face set in a grimace like a tribal war mask, knees bent deeply, fingers flared, she lunged across the room.

Mom's recurring illnesses and lack of education kept her in menial jobs, but she made it clear to my sisters and me that we could do whatever we wanted. "Do what makes you happy and everything else will fall into place." And nothing, it seemed, made Sue happier than dancing at bars in The City. She disappeared after dinner every night and returned long after the house was asleep, crashing around before settling with a sigh into her bed.

One day she brought home a friend. Unlike Sue, Anita wore makeup and a feminine blouse. Her shake was firm but warm. I liked her instantly.

As I sat upstairs with them, I noted that Anita called my sister Susan, not Sue, or Susie. It was a grown-up name, spoken by someone that knew her in a different way. Sue settled in against the bed and closed her eyes and Anita gently rubbed her shoulders. I never touched my friends like that.

As a child Sue was petite and pretty; but, annoyed that my brothers weren't more masculine, she became a tomboy. She also was better at baseball and football than they were. She never liked playing with dolls, except to cut off their hair (early practice for her current hair styling business?) and hated dressing up.

Later that afternoon, I walked into the kitchen and caught them embracing by the stove. They looked ashamed as their arms fell to their sides. I padded quickly upstairs. I accepted the fact that Glenn was gay. Why should I feel any different about Sue being with another woman? Maybe by changing the subject, I could show them I was cool with their relationship. I leafed through an *Art Forum* magazine and found photos of interesting architecture in India. Tucking it under my arm, I returned to the kitchen.

"Look at how amazing these buildings are!" I blurted. They eyed me warily as I approached. Had I not understood what had happened?

I met their gaze without flinching.

"Peg, are you all right with us being together?" Sue asked.

I shrugged. Glenn never asked how I felt about him being with another man, and that was just fine with me. I didn't want to talk about it. It was what it was.

"Peg, I'm sorry. We didn't intend to burden you with this," Anita added.

"Anita and I are moving in together next week," Sue added.

"I'm fine, you guys," I said smiling. And I was, although I couldn't help wondering what other surprises my family might have in store.

* * *

"I don't think I'm going back to school next semester," Pat said nonchalantly at dinner while visiting a couple of weeks later.

Mom looked stunned. "Pat, you've only got one more year. Just finish your degree." The exasperation in her tone was unusual: she rarely questioned our decisions. Although Pat had a scholarship, Mom and Dad had worked hard to help pay for his living expenses so he could stay in school.

"Mom, what's the point?" Pat's forehead scar was no longer angry red. His hazel eyes were clear. "People either like my art or they don't. My having a degree won't make a damn bit of difference."

Mom sighed and stubbed out her cigarette longer than necessary.

Dad brought his dish to the sink. It was easier for him to be confrontational from a distance. "Pat, finish out the year, for Christ's sake."

"Dad," Pat said, turning to face him, "I'll get a job. Eventually, I'd like to make a living selling my art. I just don't think I can learn any more about art at school."

Dad shook his head and walked out of the kitchen.

* * *

Pat and five other guys moved into a turn-of-the-century house in Berkeley. Shortly thereafter, to my excitement, he invited us to a costume party.

Joan dressed as a *Hullabaloo* dancer in Mom's brown wig, short skirt, and white go-go boots. I wore a long black dress I'd bought at the Goodwill Store and went as a blonde Katherine Hepburn.

"I'm so glad you guys are here!" Pat dashed up in a Roman toga. He led me into the kitchen and showed me how to make

119

mulled wine. "Just stir it while it heats up," he said before flying off again.

Joan's laughter drifted in from the foyer as the guests arrived. She was signing them in. I peeked through the kitchen door. Flocks of handsome men stood in line. Each time one moved forward, Joan handed them the feather pen and guest book. It didn't matter that most of them were gay—Joan flirted anyway. Many flirted back.

"*Dahling*, you look divine," a young Nureyev wanna-be in Roman toga with big red lips said as he kissed Joan on both cheeks. "You will be joining us later, won't you?" Before Joan could answer he was pulled into the living room by a man wearing a loincloth. Joan was enjoying herself. I remembered her raving about the raucous drag shows she and Sue had seen in San Francisco with Glenn and Pat just a few months earlier. She appeared in the kitchen doorway, wig askew and face covered with kiss marks in varying shades of red. "If I meet one more Betty or Judy I'm going to scream!" The two of us sat down at the kitchen table with cups of mulled wine.

"I'd kill for one of those!" a deep-voiced transvestite in shocking pink skirt and short tuxedo jacket said. He was tall with hairy legs. I scurried to the stove and ladled a cup, feeling woozy as I handed it to him. Apparently, I'd done a wee too much tasting.

Joan put out her hand. "I'm Joan, Pat's sister. Aren't you one of the Cockettes?"

The man smiled coquettishly. His voice was suddenly higher. "I am indeed. You've been?"

Joan, starstruck, sat up straighter. "Yes! It was fabulous!"

When I stood to go with them to the dance floor, the room began to spin. Was it from the wine or from the dizzying pace at which my world was changing? It was becoming obvious to me that Patrick was gay, too. Would Joan soon announce she was a lesbian? Unlike Glenn, Pat didn't quote Rosalind Russell or Betty Davis. He'd always had girlfriends. Patrick had always seemed so *male.* If he and Sue could be gay, maybe I was too. I held on to the table to catch my balance.

Sue had arrived, and now spun across the hardwood floor in bare feet. Dressed in headscarf, billowing skirt, and peasant top, she looked as if she'd stepped out of the Vermeer-style painting Pat had hung above our fireplace. But the rapture the girl showed in the painting had nothing on the rapture on Sue's face as she got down with her bad self *all over* that living room floor.

When Mary Wells's song "Two Lovers" came on, many young men grouped into threes, holding hands, swaying as they sang. Joan was dating Dan again, Sue was seeing Anita, and my brothers had no shortage of admirers. Where was someone for me? I glanced around the room. Sprinkled in with all the young men were a few young women. Although some of them were pretty, they did nothing for me. I definitely preferred men. But nothing I could do would make these men interested in me.

"*Ooooo … ooooo … ooooo,*" the Stones' "Gimme Shelter" blared. People shouted. I joined Joan á la go-go and the Cockette on the dance floor. We laughed with wild abandon as our steps and the throbbing music made the floor shake. A vase fell from a table. Books scooted off shelves. I did a turn. Someone in Cleopatra wig and heavy eyeliner was heading my way. I stared in disbelief. It was Glenn. He was absolutely beautiful. He waved regally from across the room, his gold lame dress sashaying as he moved. Sidling in beside us on the dance floor, he snapped his fingers as he swayed with small, controlled hip movements. For her part, on the crowded floor, Joan took up plenty of room, her hips swinging wide. Soon Sue and Pat were swing dancing to the rock and roll beat inside our whirling circle of steps, counter-steps, laughter, and haughty expressions.

I felt envy and pride as attractive young men sent adoring glances my brothers' way. *If it can't be me, I'm glad it's them.* I closed my eyes, feverishly dancing to the pulsing rhythm. "You Can't Always Get What You Want …" the Stones intoned. Life was a roller coaster. I might as well hang on and enjoy the ride.

Chapter 14

Sailors Take Warning

August, 1970

I had started dating a fellow who went by the nickname "Buzz." He was good looking with wiry brown hair, had a great sense of humor; and true to his name, he drove a motorcycle. I was nuzzling Buzz at a pizza parlor one night when I felt someone's eyes boring into me. Though my vision was blurry (I still refused to wear glasses) I could make out Paul sitting with his friends at a table behind us. I waved. He waved back, but didn't smile. He was jealous! I knew the feeling. It still pained me to see him with any other girl.

A few weeks later, a car slowed next to me as I walked home from school. I steeled myself: would it be a put down or an attempted pick up? I looked straight ahead and kept walking.

My breaths became shorter. I walked faster. The car sped up. I stopped. The car came to a halt.

"Holy shit, the car's on fire!" a familiar voice screamed. Paul and his friend Dean flung open the doors of Dean's '63 Impala and ran for the trunk. Flames shot out as they forced open the trunk. Dean, apprenticing with his father as a plumber, had chemicals stored back there.

"My dad's gonna kill me!" Dean shouted. He grabbed towels from the backseat and patted down the flames.

"So," Paul said laughing as he turned to me, "you wanna ride home?"

I laughed. "Do I dare?"

Paul grabbed a couple of smaller clean towels from the backseat and gave one to me, to cover our noses. Paul sat in the front seat and I sat in the back. I tried not to notice the curls at the nape of his neck.

"Goddamn it!" Dean was beyond caring about the health effects of the fumes in the car. He banged the steering wheel with his hand.

I tried to ignore the physical effect on me of Paul's masculine walk when he escorted me to the front door. "Is it okay if I call you?" he asked, looking into my eyes. His arm brushed mine, and a spark ignited in the pit of my stomach. *Pull me in ...* My desire to be with him cut through my fear of being dumped again. I brushed some ash from his shirt. "Sure," I smiled.

Though he was training for the upcoming football season, Paul found time to call. He picked me up in his red MG sports car, and we drove in the hills along Redwood Road.

"I'm pretty busy with football and stuff," Paul said before leaving. He wanted to see me, but didn't have time, his words implied.

"That's okay. I'm pretty busy, too." I was enjoying being on the school dance committee and in the Drama and Russian clubs.

Two weeks later, Paul dislocated his knee in football practice and was put in a cast up to his hip. He called me the next day. "Remember how I said I was too busy? Well, I'm not anymore." Suddenly, he had all the time in the world, and he wanted to spend it with me.

I cut back on my after-school activities. Soon we were spending all of our free time together again. Now that we were older, kissing was no longer enough. Though we came very close to breaking my vow of not having sex until I was eighteen, one of us always held firm that we shouldn't go all the way. I have to admit that it wasn't always me.

* * *

January, 1971

Glenn wanted to teach French, so just after Christmas, he left to study at the University of Grenoble. Now living in San Francisco, Pat had made a connection with a gallery owner and was working on paintings for an upcoming show. Sue shared an apartment in Oakland with Anita, and crammed dance classes in between shifts as a waitress. Joan had classes in art and anthropology at Cal. Whether I liked it or not, my siblings had begun living independent lives.

Paul drove me to school. Sometimes he'd pick me up early, and we'd get coffee and a Danish at Denny's. One morning, as we sat across from each other sipping coffee, I noticed he hadn't touched his pastry. I asked what was wrong.

"My dad left last night," he said quietly.

"Where'd he go?" I asked innocently.

"No, I mean he *left* left—moved out." Paul took a deep breath and stared at the table.

I was floored. His family didn't do things like that. Only mine did. *"Why?"*

He said haltingly, "He's been seeing another woman. None of us, including Mom, had any idea." I moved across the booth next to him and took his hand.

* * *

On the days that Dad was at work Danny's footsteps pattered softly down the stairs in the early morning hours as he slipped out of the house. Mom woke up early; no doubt she heard the footsteps too. Other mothers would have had a fit if their daughter's boyfriend slept over, but not mine. Joan was over eighteen, on birth control, and happy. To Mom, that was all that mattered. She and Dad had no idea why Dan had been discharged; they only knew that it had been "honorable." They hadn't been there the year before when Dan, home on leave and dealing weed, had laid out more ziplock baggies of pot than I could count on Joan's bed. I gasped and Joan giggled—we'd never seen so much grass!

That spring, Dan decided to move to Susanville, a city in the mountains of Northern California. Joan didn't want to go, saying she wanted to continue her studies at Cal. But each time Joan made the five-hour drive to visit him on weekends she returned home distracted, as though part of her had been left behind.

* * *

Summer, 1971

In June, Glenn sent me a postcard from Morocco. He'd befriended an older American writer who had a palatial Moorish villa in Tangier. Though he "felt like Aladdin in the palace of

125

Ali Baba," he wrote, he moved in. The friend invited him to be his companion on an excursion through India, Ceylon (now Sri Lanka) and Nepal. After that, he'd return to Grenoble to continue his studies, so he wouldn't be home for a while. In closing, he wrote: "I can't believe you're going to be a senior! Give 'em hell, Pegs, and have fun!" I smiled as I studied the postcard showing white houses dotting a hillside overlooking the bay of Tangier.

Joan's weekends in Susanville were turning into weeks, and in August, she announced she'd be moving there after all. In 1971, lots of moms objected to their daughters moving in with their boyfriends. Not mine. "Live with a man before you marry him, girls," was my mom's adage. Dad didn't object. He liked that Dan had been in the navy, thinking, perhaps, that he'd be a good steady man to steer Joan through life's choppy waters. Little did he know.

If Mom and Dad *had* objected I couldn't picture them telling Joan "No." There was a good reason why Mom had nicknamed Joan "The Boss." When she made up her mind, we all jumped out of her way. When Mom merely suggested that Joan finish up at Cal Berkeley Joan responded brusquely, "I can always take classes at the Mt. Lassen Junior College."

Joan had always loved Cal. Now she was willing to go from UC Berkeley to a junior college out in the middle of nowhere? What else was she willing to give up for Danny? Before she left, I asked Joan what Susanville was like.

"Everywhere you go, it smells like pine. A lot of hippies from the Bay Area have moved there. There's not a lot to do, but that's okay. It's kind of nice to just be surrounded by nature— you know—like Thoreau." Joan liked hiking, but she also liked hanging out in coffeehouses and going to The City. It seemed to me that she was trying to convince herself that she liked it. Danny's dreams were becoming hers. Her own dreams were already fading away.

* * *

November, 1971

Mom slid bobby pins from her hair and set them on her dresser and then pulled off her brown wig and put it on its Styrofoam head next to the bobby pins. Its blank face stared at me. Mom sat down on her bed and lit a cigarette. I sat on the floor nearby and leaned against the wall.

"Well, little one, how's life?" Mom asked. She was always ready these days to have a conversation, no matter how big the subject. After all, I was the only bird left in the nest.

"Life's good. I just got all my college applications out," I replied.

"And how do you like your new class?" That semester I'd taken an advanced high school study class of my choice at UC Berkeley. Ever since I'd discovered the higher truths on Sue's wall, I'd had a fascination with Eastern thought. I'd chosen "Religions of India."

"I love it!" I enthused.

Mom smiled. "And you and Paul are doing okay?"

"Yep ..." I replied, my voice trailing off.

"I'm glad you're finally letting the poor boy in the house," she said with a laugh as she fluffed up the wisps of hair above her forehead. She wiped some denture cream from the corner of her mouth. The year before, she'd finally paid off our dental bills and gone to the dentist herself. Apparently, her teeth were a mess. She decided to have the whole lot of them pulled and got dentures. She was forty-eight. I missed her Mother Rabbit front teeth. First, the wig replaced her real hair; now she had these teeth that looked like everyone else's. She feathered her cigarette ashes along the side of the ashtray, a sign that she was waiting for me to speak. She seemed to know that I needed to talk.

Paul and I *were* fine. We'd grown closer over the past year. As he shared the details of his parents' breakup, I finally felt comfortable disclosing my family's secrets. He didn't judge them as I once feared. He seemed to like them for who they were. Sharing our stories had made our relationship stronger. But I was starting to feel stifled.

Even though I'd cut back on helping with school dances and doing fund-raisers for Drama and Russian Club, Paul still complained. "Do you have to sign up for *everything?*" But why couldn't I spend time with him *and* do these other things?

"Maybe Paul and I got back together again too soon," I said to my mother now, wrapping my arms around my knees. "He says I'm always busy when he wants to do something."

"Do what *you* need to do, honey. Paul may not like it, but he'll stick around." She tapped her ashes into the ashtray and looked up, "Honey, you're just like me."

And just like that, my feeling of being pressured by Paul went away.

Many times over the years, Mom had compared me to herself; I had taken it as her way of empathizing with me. Now I really thought about it. She was the youngest in her family, and so was I. So was Daddy, and so was Paul. Mom and Dad had been childhood sweethearts, like Paul and me. She had been active in high school, and, like me, she'd had a lot of friends.

A chill ran through me at my next thought. I jumped to my feet. At nineteen, Mom had had her first nervous breakdown. I found myself screaming, "*No! I'm **not** just like you!*"

Mom looked shaken. I'd never raised my voice to her before.

"*I'm ME! I'll never be like you!*" I ran out of the room and leaped up the stairs. I stared into my eyes in the bathroom mirror. My eyes were still and my pupils looked normal. Nana, I'd heard, had been institutionalized, too. Had Mom stood at her mirror when she was my age, studying her eye movements, going pale at the thought of going crazy like her mother? I'd be nineteen in two years. Would I begin to sink, too, the way my mother did in my dream, sitting with bound hands in a rowboat disappearing beneath the waves?

Growing up, I'd heard that mental illness was an inheritable disease and that one in five children of people diagnosed with mental illness might expect to develop it. But I didn't need to read any scientific studies about it to know this disease was inherited: not only was Mom's mother mentally ill, but when I was thirteen, Mom's sister Marie, four years her senior and in her early forties, had her first bout of mental illness and had to be hospitalized. Since there were four kids in Mom's family, our strain of mental illness seemed particularly rabid, with a 50 percent inheritable rate. What was worse, the danger period wasn't over in your late teens: if you happened to be predisposed to get it, stress and major life changes could bring it on at any time through middle age.

Somehow, we already knew what recent studies have shown: that madness and creativity are two sides of the same hand, both a result of being more open to stimuli streaming in. We definitely had the genes. We knew what we didn't want: to go crazy like Mom. But there was nothing the five of us aspired to more—not good looks or intellect or success—than being creative. The trick was being able to live a creative life without going crazy.

Chapter 15

❧❧

A Cozy Cottage

May, 1972

I looked out the window to see Joan was getting out of a snow-white BMW. I ran down the stairs and out the front door.

"Hey, Peg," Joan said nonchalantly. She hugged me before slinging her bag over her shoulder. She'd come to stay the weekend.

"Whose car is *this*?" I ran my hand over the smooth metal.

"Isn't it pretty? Dan bought it," Joan beamed.

Danny bought a beamer on his pay at the army depot? I was doubtful, but said nothing.

Joan's voice was matter-of-fact. "With all the driving we'll be doing between here and Susanville he thought we better get a dependable car." She walked over to the mailbox and pulled out the mail.

"There's something for you from Mills College." she handed me a packet, a look of curiosity on her face. Mills was the college I'd dreamed of attending. It was a green oasis in Oakland just off Highway 580, with walking bridges over streams and paths lined with eucalyptus trees. I'd applied even though I knew my parents couldn't afford the tuition. Maybe a miracle would happen.

My stomach jumped. Joan watched as I opened the packet.

"I got accepted!" I said. I ran inside to show Mom. She'd grown up in Oakland. In her day, Mills was a school for women from wealthy families. It would have been the kind of school she'd have liked to attend, if things had turned out differently for her.

Mom was in the kitchen making meat loaf. But instead of cheering *"Attagirl,* Peg, I knew you could do it!" when I showed her the letter, she sighed and pursed her lips. "Honey, we can't afford to send you to Mills. Even with the kids getting scholarships, we can barely afford the University of California."

"I know, Mom. I just thought you'd be excited that I got in." I tried not to sound dejected. I went upstairs.

Joan's lilting laughter drifted up the stairs. A few minutes later, she flung the door open, paper in hand.

"Peg, you dumb dodo, they're giving you *a full scholarship.* All you have to pay is $59 the first semester, and $78 the second."

I grabbed the financial aid letter from her hand. Leave it to Joan to read the whole packet!

"Egetha, you little dickens: a full scholarship to Mills! How in the world did you manage *that?*" Mom was behind her, her face flushed with excitement.

Mom went back to her bed, poured herself a celebratory cup of lukewarm coffee and lit a cigarette. She smiled broadly and took my hand as I came in to sit down on the end of her bed. *"Attagirl,* Peg, Atagirl."

* * *

June, 1972

Joan came home again for my high school graduation, as did Sue and Pat. Glenn was completing his studies at the University of Grenoble and couldn't come. Mom's locomotive stilettos made sure they got my family seats near the front for the ceremony.

* * *

September, 1972

I turned eighteen the last week of September. Paul and I drove to Tahoe that weekend to stay at his brother's condo and have sex. I'd started taking the pill a few weeks before. More nervous than passionate that first time after building the event up for so long, it seemed that we were both relieved to have the deed done. With practice and relaxation over the ensuing weeks and months we got the hang of it, and made a habit of doing it whenever possible. Our bodies, we decided, were a perfect fit.

* * *

October, 1972

I was studying my biology text for my Tuesday morning Mills class on the living room couch when Dad, still in work uniform, came in the front door smiled tightly and nodded before heading for his bedroom. Firemen worked shifts that lasted several days in a row: he wasn't due back home for a couple of days.

I went to find Mom in the kitchen. "Why's Dad home?"

"He's got problems at work, honey," Mom's voice became deeper when she whispered. "They're asking questions about an inspection he did a couple of years ago." By 1960, Dad had advanced to being a community liaison, doing fire safety demonstrations at local schools, events, and on television (sometimes, we even saw him on Captain Kangaroo!). Now he was a fire investigator, examining sites for safety. Apparently, there had been a fire at a location that he had reported as safe.

The next few months were tense. Dad tried to appear upbeat, but when he settled down at the table with the paper, he stared absently into space.

* * *

June, 1973

College that year was everything I'd hoped, with small classes and easy access to professors even for required undergraduate courses. I learned to juggle studying so that I could spend time with Paul. He was thrilled that I decided to go to a women's college (no chance of my wanting to date classmates) but, as before, he was aggravated at how preoccupied I always seemed. Couldn't I just read that philosophy book the next morning before class and go to a movie that night instead? He'd obviously never read Ayn Rand. He was at the nearby junior college, studying to become a policeman. But by the end of the school year, he, like my father many years before, decided that it wasn't for him. Most of the guys in the class, he said, seemed more interested in arresting people than helping people. Though Paul continued taking classes toward a general degree, he also began working part time at his family's steel fabricating business. His weekends were spent racing Motocross.

The week after school ended, Joan called to say she was coming down to pick up some things. Would I like to come up to Susanville for a week? With Paul preoccupied with his racing, my answer was a swift and guilt-free "Yes!"

I jumped in the front passenger seat of the BMW and threw my bag in the back. Joan grabbed a cassette from the glove box and Marvin Gaye started singing, "Oh Mercy Mercy Me ... Things Ain't What They Used to Be ..." When we reached the mountains, Joan rolled down her window, stuck her head out like a dog, and took a deep whiff of the pine air. "God, I love that smell! You see that cluster of trees?" she said, pointing to the right. "Those are Ponderosa Pines, they're my favorite. They get real tall and grow in families." Did I detect a southern twang in Joan's voice? She'd dropped the "ly" from the word "really." She sounded like a mountain hippie. Even her diction was fading away!

Joan exited the highway, and the landscape became rural. Children ran through sheets and towels hung from a clothesline in front of a house with a sagging roof. A narrow road led us to a cottage surrounded by wildflowers.

"Here we are," she smiled. I got out of the car and took a deep breath. Joan was right—the smell was delicious.

Joan's black lab thumped his tail as she kneeled to pet him. She waved at a woman in the doorway of another cottage across from us. "That's Karen, one of our renters."

"You own that place?" I asked, dumbfounded.

"Well, Dan does. He bought it when he bought our house."

The side door squeaked as we walked inside. The kitchen had knotty pine walls and an old stove like Grandma's that smelled of bacon. Joan frowned at the pile of dishes in the sink.

I sat at the kitchen table while Joan brought our bags to her room. On her way back she picked up the random men's shirts, jeans, and socks on the floor and dropped them on the washing machine in the corner of the kitchen.

"Make yourself at home, Peg," she said. Her gaze fell on a vase of flowers on the table. In front of the vase was a note: "Welcome home, Joanie Pies. See ya later, love, Me." Joan shook her head and smiled. "Charmer."

Having twisted her long, blonde hair into a knot, she clipped it atop her head, put a record on the stereo, and swayed to the Aretha Franklin music as she scrubbed the dishes. The ballet class she'd been taking at the local junior college had improved her posture. With her hair up, she looked like a prima ballerina auditioning for *Soul Train*.

She put the last of the dishes to dry in the rack, wiped the counter, and opened the cupboard next to the sink to put the coffee away. She made room on the shelf by moving some glass jars that were filled with long dark sticks that looked like some kind of spice.

"Is that cinnamon?" I asked.

"Oh," she said scowling, "that's Danny's Thai stick." Paul and I smoked it before with them. Dan put only a tiny bit of it in a pipe, and we were so loaded we thought we were walking on our knees. That was a ton of Thai!

I thought back to Dan's baggies of pot on Joan's bed. Then it had seemed like a game. Now Joan kept Thai stick next to her coffee in the cupboard. I shivered involuntarily.

* * *

September, 1973 to January, 1974

In my sophomore year at Mills, I got a bussing job in the Tea Shop for $1.65 an hour and shared a cottage with a school friend, Sue Rockwell. It was $100 a month. Sue and I decorated the place with our artwork and stacked our books and albums on wood planks balanced on cement blocks. Neither one of us owned a TV.

Since Sue's mom had found the place, Sue got the only bedroom and I squeezed a bed onto the back porch. "Where do you want to be when you're thirty?" Sue asked one evening. Sitting on the couch across from me in striped knee-high socks, her wiry red hair divided into pigtails, she looked like Pippi Longstocking.

It was a delicious question. "I don't know … living in The City or in a monastery in Nepal," I said giddily imagining myself standing on a ledge, arms outstretched, looking out at the Himalayan mountains. I was free as a bird! Suddenly, my tenth-grade English teacher, Mrs. Dickie, who'd taught most of my family, appeared beside me on the ledge in sensible shoes and black pointed glasses. Taking my arm, she admonished "What about those Kennedy genes, Peg?"

Meanwhile my siblings' lives were moving into high gear. After two years of study and travel, Glenn came home. He was hired to teach an undergraduate course in French at UC Berkeley and found a studio apartment near the campus. Sue was hand-picked by the renowned dancer, Bella Lewitsky, to attend the prestigious School of Dance at the California Institute for the Arts, and moved with Anita to Southern California. Pat created a line of hand-painted animal and human masks that everyone from Ringo Starr to Cher had to have on their walls. Joan's graphic design business in Susanville was thriving. I felt pretty boring next to them.

So when Sasa, a friend from Mills, asked me to come to Greece to be in her wedding that summer after my sophomore year, I jumped at the chance. Mom and Dad, like saints come down from heaven, pitched in $500 from their tax return. I had no trouble picturing their holy cards: Dad would have a full head of hair, and Mom would be smoking a cigarette.

* * *

August, 1974

The weekend after I got home, I went along with the other girlfriends to watch Paul and his buddies jump and turn as they sped around the Motocross track, the engines whining and tires kicking up dirt. Although the sport *was* exciting, and I was proud of Paul when he won: it was his adventure, not mine.

Though Paul and I still communicated effortlessly with our bodies, we no longer seemed to speak the same language. My experiences had given me new insight into the world and who I was. He didn't seem to like the new me.

At dinner one night a week after I got home, Mom smoked while I stared at the meat loaf, mashed potatoes and corn nibbles (in Greece, I had begun eating meat again) as I waited for Dad to join us. "Go ahead and eat, Peg. I'll wait for Daddy," Mom said, feathering her ashes on the side of the ashtray.

Soon, Dad walked in, raising his eyebrows as he sat to show he was okay. He lifted his plate absently for Mom to fill. His eyes opened wide when he chewed, as though the meat loaf was rubbery; an attempt at humor. Mom set her cigarette down and clasped her hands together like a church and steeple. The steeple folded back into the church as she turned to Dad. "Jack, it's okay. We can talk about it, honey," she said as if to a child after a bad dream.

Dad moved his corn around on his plate. He blinked several times.

"Mom, it's all right. Dad doesn't need to talk," I said. It was too painful to see my father so nervous and subdued.

"Jack," Mom asked tenderly, "would it be easier if *I* told Peg?"

Dad nodded, closed his eyes, and clenched his jaw.

"Daddy lost his job at the firehouse today," Mom said quietly.

I put my hand over my mouth.

"Twenty-four years working for The City of Oakland and they fire him just months before his twenty-five year retirement." Mom was white with anger.

I thought back to the last time Dad had problems with work. "They fired him because of one bad report?" I asked, stunned.

"They said I was drinking." Dad rubbed his forehead. "I slurred my words during a presentation and fell off the stage."

Mom and Dad might have a couple of drinks on the weekends, but I'd never known Daddy to take a drink during the week.

"*Were* you drinking, Dad?" I asked.

Dad shook his head, but was silent.

"Uncle Russ says he knows damn well Daddy wouldn't drink on the job. He thinks he had a stroke, and that The City is trying to avoid paying the higher twenty-five-year pension." Mom furiously twirled her cigarette butt around the ashtray. "Russ really thinks you need to have a doctor's exam and take The City of Oakland to court." She squeezed Dad's hand. "I do too, honey."

Dad pulled in his lips, which gave his mouth an uneven look, and shook his head. "I'm not going to fight it."

Dad's years in the army and with the police and fire departments had trained him not to question authority. He was a good soldier. He would not protest.

* * *

Two months later, Mom, just home from her new job at another employment agency, entered the kitchen in robe and slippers. It was 5:30 p.m.

"How was your day, Egetha?" she asked brightly.

I closed my book and sighed. "Fine, but I'll be happy when this semester's over."

She lit a cigarette and exhaled. "Honey, we're going to have to sell the house."

My heart skipped. *Sell the house!* The house had been our home for over ten years, longer than we'd lived anywhere else. "Why?"

"Honey, we just can't afford to pay the property taxes with Daddy's skimpy pension." I had a guilty thought. *That $500 Mom and Dad gave me for Greece would have come in handy.*

The water in the pot on the stove boiled. Mom dropped in some spaghetti. I set the table, taking special care to fold the napkins and line the forks and knives up with the plates. The camellias outside the kitchen window were vibrant in pink and red. *Nothing lasts forever. Life is change. Change is good.* I repeated the Buddhist mantra, wanting desperately to believe it.

Chapter 16

❦

The People's Car

September, 1974

My friend and former roommate Sue transferred to UC Riverside, so I searched for a place of my own. Mom and Dad sold the house and were moving to an apartment. I needed a car but had spent all my money on my trip to Greece. Two high-pitched honks sounded out my bedroom window to see Paul getting out of a green Volkswagen. I ran outside.

"Come see your new car," he said, grinning as he took my hand.

I was speechless.

"Sorry, the paint's a little bubbly in some places. I should have had them sand it before they repainted it," he said sheepishly.

"I love it!" I said, squeezing him hard before jumping behind the wheel. *My own car!*

I pushed in the clutch and turned the key. "*Rrrr ...*"

"You need to try it a couple of times before it'll start. I'll take it in to have the ignition checked," Paul said apologetically.

"That's okay," I said and turned the key again. "*Rrr ... rrrr ... rrrrhummm.*" I smiled. "I'll call it *Rrr*oger."

The following week, someone at Mills offered to sublet her Berkeley studio to me for six months. I couldn't believe my good fortune. The studio had a sunny kitchen, its own yard, and was only $100 a month. I decorated it in my own style, with a bentwood rocker and lamp with a palm frond shade. Though it wasn't in San Francisco, I was getting closer. But the six months whizzed by too quickly.

Though I was now making more money ($2.35 an hour— the minimum wage was $2.75) working as a clerk in the Mills business office, I was unable to find a place I could afford on my own. So I was relieved when my friend Joni asked me to move into her brand-new apartment in Walnut Creek.

Joni and I did our best to make the sterile apartment hip with loads of plants and a red Mylar dragon kite floating from the living room to the back bedroom. It wasn't San Francisco, but it had two bedrooms. I hung masks that Patrick had made alongside my sketches on the walls. It would do for now.

* * *

June, 1975

Paul was socking away money, working full time at his family's steel fabricating company while living at home with his mom, but he itched to move out. That June, he bought a new condo not far from where I was living with Joni and asked me to move in with him. But I wasn't ready. "Live with a man before you marry him," Mom had said. And what about living in The

City? Paul's condo sat empty while he waited for me to change my mind. Then he asked Dean to move in with him.

Paul was now racing both Friday and Saturday nights, which meant the only time we had together was during the week when I had to study. If he hadn't placed well at the races, he remained irritable during the week. We had become a miserable pair.

By January, I was dating other guys.

* * *

May, 1976

Having perfected the fine art of procrastination, I was frantically trying to complete my senior thesis and classes while working more hours in the business office. The woman who handled student accounts was leaving, and I hoped to take over her job after graduation. That way, I could save enough money to earn a Master's degree in Asian Studies and teach at a college nearby.

On the day of my graduation from Mills, my parents sat with my brothers and sisters a few rows back from the stage. When they announced my name, my siblings whooped and Mom and Dad grinned from ear to ear. Though I was still seeing someone else, my parents invited Paul, who they still considered part of the family, to their after-graduation party for me. I chose not to invite my boyfriend: with Paul there, it would only create problems.

I was thrilled when I got the job in the business office. Although Paul and I stayed in touch, I was still dating other people. Paul apparently thought it was time I stopped.

One afternoon in June, I got a call at work from my roommate, Joni. "Uh, Peg, Paul's here ... Uh ... he's moving your stuff to his condo."

"He's *what?*" I ranted. "*Tell him not to touch my things!*"

"Uh ... it's too late..." Joni replied nervously. "He's already taken all of it."

When I arrived, Paul was carrying the last of my shoes from his trunk up the stairs to his condo.

"What in the hell are you doing?" I asked.

"No. I did," he replied with finality.

"Get your racing buddies to move in with you!"

"I want you," he said earnestly. He looked comical, with my flats and sneakers poking from the top of the carton box he carried.

"I can't believe Joni let you do this."

"She said it was romantic." He smiled.

"I'm moving back in with my parents! Don't bother to call me!" I screamed as I closed my car door. People had gathered in the grassy area near the pool to watch. They seemed to be enjoying this. I turned the key. "*Rrrrrrr ...*" Everyone's eyes were on me. I hissed and turned it again. "*Rrrrrrrr ... rrrrrrrrrr ... rrrrrrrrrrr.*" I hit the steering wheel, pumped the gas pedal, pushed in and out the clutch, and turned it again. "*Rrrrrrrrhhhhhummmmm ...*"

I didn't wave good-bye.

* * *

Though I managed to get my clothes and shoes back from Paul, he held on to my furniture and artwork. I didn't need them at my folks' place, anyway.

I continued seeing my boyfriend, but our interest in each other gradually fizzled. When Paul asked me out on a date one night, we had drinks around the pool with some friends he'd made from the condominium complex. It was fun. After dinner, as we snuggled together in the comfort of his waterbed, I said "Yes" again. We still fit.

By September, Paul had cut back on his racing. In October, I moved into his condo. One sacrifice deserved another. Some day soon, I promised myself, I'd talk Paul into moving to San Francisco. For now, we could dress up the suburban condo to give it some style. We put jungle-themed wallpaper in bright orange, yellow, and green in the kitchen and roof shingles on the living room and bedroom walls. My bentwood rocker and lamp with palm frond shade fit nicely in the living room. But my sketches seemed out of place on the condo's white walls. I left them rolled up in the guest bedroom closet next to my wooden box of art supplies. I was losing interest in being creative, anyway. After awhile, I forgot they were there.

* * *

In March 1977, after five years of living together, Joan and Dan were married in a civil ceremony in Susanville. I was shocked. Wasn't this the couple that said marriage was just a piece of paper?

If Joan could get married, I could, too. Paul and I decided to get married on the first of October. I should have consulted my arbiter of good taste, Patrick, before choosing the colors that send viewers of our wedding album into paroxysms of laughter: peach-colored bridesmaid dresses and rust-colored tuxes with ruffled peach shirts.

* * *

July, 1977

Mom and Dad were glad they could formally welcome Paul into our family. At the same time, Mom, dusting off her go-go boots, was antsy for a change. Now that Paul and I were getting married, she and Dad would find an apartment in Walnut Creek. That way, they could spend more time with us as well as with her brother Jack and his wife Lauretta, who lived in nearby Concord. With no children to worry about, the four of them could spend endless amiable hours chatting with cocktails by the pool.

But just days after my parents unpacked their dishes Mom received a tearful call from Lauretta: her brother's heart had suddenly given out. He was gone.

Two weeks later Mom lit a cigarette as her crossed leg swung her Ked shoe like a pendulum back and forth under my kitchen table. It may as well have been a white go-go boot. Dad had taken a night job as a security guard to augment his pension, and she didn't want to stay home alone. Taking a sip of coffee from the cup I'd just set in front of her she exclaimed, "Gosh, I don't know, Peg, if I were getting married today, I wouldn't know where to buy the dress, let alone anything else."

I hadn't asked her where to buy a dress. I already bought one and had shown it to her months before.

"Thanks, Mom, but I think I have it taken care of." I nodded and smiled uneasily. Maybe it was just that her medication needed a little tweaking.

"Lord, I could use a cigarette, let alone anything else."

There was that phrase again. But this time, it didn't make any sense. She held a burning Benson and Hedges in her hand. Then there was the poor diction. That wasn't Mom. Her eyes took a few two-steps. My heart jumped. Repetitive phrases were a sure sign that Mom was teetering at the edge of sanity.

The next day, I called Dad. "Has Mom stopped taking her medication?"

"Your mother's on a new medication called Lithium, Peg. They warned me that it might take her a while to adjust."

During that so-called adjustment period, Mom got the bug to drive up to Susanville to visit Joan. I was concerned: it had been years since she'd driven farther than the grocery store. But Joan gave Mom directions, and Mom arrived on Joan's doorstep, small pink suitcase in hand. At first, Joan liked having Mom there. By the second day, however, Mom's excessive use of the phrase "let alone anything else" began to worry Joan and Dan to distraction. They were relieved when Mom was too tired to go with them to the movies, but when they got home, Mom and her car were gone. A few minutes later, there was a knock on their door: the police.

The next morning, a Sunday, Joan called me at 6:00 a.m. "You're flying up to Reno now to drive Mom home," she said bossily. "Mom drove up Main Street in her underwear last night yelling, 'I'm free as a bird,' out her window. Two very nice policemen brought her back here."

I knew better than to argue. Though I felt guilty for not warning Joan about that suspicious phrase before Mom went, I thanked God she'd flipped out in Susanville instead of Walnut Creek. "Okay, but you're driving back with us," I countered. "I can't handle her on my own."

I hung up the phone. "I have to fly to Reno," I said casually to Paul as he opened his bleary eyes.

"If your mom could drive up there, can't she just drive herself back?" he asked.

"It's hard to explain." I hurriedly put on my clothes while trying to stay matter-of-fact with Paul. "When Mom was on Thorazine I knew what to expect. Once she started to go, it was only a few days before she was completely gone. I'm not sure yet what to expect from Lithium." Thankfully, he didn't ask any more questions because I didn't have any more answers.

Mom was all smiles when she and Joan met me at the Reno airport.

"We're going to have such fun!" she said, overly buoyant. My stomach sank. Joan and I exchanged wary glances as we climbed into the front seat of the car.

"Go ahead and spread out Mom. Take a nap if you like. It's a long drive back to my house," Joan said.

As Mom nodded off, I prayed that she would sleep until we were back in the Bay Area. As we wound down the mountain highway from Reno, the temperature soared. Since we didn't have air conditioning, we rolled down all the windows.

It had been a while since Joan and I had talked.

"How are your wedding plans going?" Joan asked quietly.

"Okay, I guess. We decided to have the wedding at Mills. It's in six weeks." I nodded at the backseat. *Six more weeks.* The vague panic that had first surfaced the week before reappeared. My stomach churned. Joan's smile was tight. She understood. *What if Mom's still crazy at my wedding?*

Mom woke up at a stoplight in Auburn. She sat rigid, her eyes darting from right to left. She ripped her wig off her head and threw it out the window. Joan stepped on the gas.

Mom ran her fingers through her hair. Since it wasn't freshly washed, it stood at attention all over her head like Medusa's snakes. She next nonchalantly removed her dentures, laying them on the seat beside her. She pulled her wallet from her purse. Before I could grab it, she threw her drivers' license out the window. Joan pushed the power buttons to roll up the windows and latched the doors.

"Shouldn't we go back to get her driver's license?" I said. The stop sign grew smaller in the rear view window.

"Not a good idea," Joan said dryly.

The temperature outside hovered at one hundred, and we had no air conditioning. My bare arms stuck to the armrest, and sweat trickled down my neck. Mom struck a match, and smoke filled the car. Joan leaned toward me. "She has to walk in to the hospital on her own," she whispered, reminding me that the guidelines for admitting people needing psychiatric care had changed.

I glanced back at Mom: she had taken a blanket from under the backseat and wrapped it around herself. We were on the road with Chief Running Bear.

I shot Joan a panicked look.

"I think we better go see Patrick," she said.

"Patrick?" I asked hopefully.

"Yep," Joan nodded emphatically. "She'll listen to him."

It was a rare sunny summer afternoon in The City, and Patrick was having a get together at his flat in lower Pacific Heights.

When Joan rang the buzzer, Pat sprinted down the stairs. "What a great surprise!" He put his arm around her shoulders.

"Um, Mom's in the car with Peg." Joan cast a yearning look at the sounds of the party from above.

"Great, let's bring 'em in!" Pat said. Instead, Joan led him to the car where I sat locked in with our mother and opened the back door. Patrick drew in a quick breath before taking our toothless, disheveled mother's hand. "Now Mother," he said, smiling as if they shared a secret, "You know something's not quite right here, don't you?" Joan and I stifled our nervous laughs behind our hands as Pat continued, "Mom, the girls are going to take you to see the doctor. Is that okay with you?"

Mom nodded and bit her lower lip with her upper gum.

"And you will do whatever the doctor says you need to do, won't you?" Pat asked.

Mom thought for a minute, then smiled a Stan Laurel smile as only someone without teeth can do. Pat laughed. "That's good," he said and patted her on the arm. "You might want to put those back in so you don't lose them." He pointed to the dentures on the backseat. Mom nodded, opened her mouth, and slipped them into place. She ran her tongue around them.

It must have been tough for Pat to walk back up those stairs to his guests and act as though nothing had happened. But we siblings were old hands at covering up mom's illnesses.

* * *

October 1, 1977

The maple trees in front of the Mills College Chapel had changed color. Small gusts of wind blew huddles of the fallen red and orange leaves past the entrance, where people were gathering. Some leaves blew down the walkway and onto the vast lawn in front of the Music Building, and a few continued farther to the large round pond, where they floated for passersby to admire.

Shaped like a hexagon with high ceilings, the chapel had a stone altar in the center in the form of a cross. Pews formed a half-circle in front of the altar while the tall spires of the organ covered the room's back wall. Eucalyptus and flowering shrubs surrounded the floor-to-ceiling windows. It was one of my favorite buildings on campus. When I couldn't get a priest to come there to marry us, I found a minister. Though Nana was upset that I wasn't having a Catholic wedding, I wasn't about to change my mind. The place was holy enough for me.

Mom dabbed her eyes as she sat in a chair near an ashtray in the corner of the "bride's room" of the chapel. Chief Running Bear had surrendered peacefully to the authorities at the psychiatric hospital and emerged three days later as my mother. Shortly thereafter, Nana broke her hip and Mom and Dad moved back to the same apartment complex they'd moved from in Castro Valley to be closer to her. While we packed up her dishes yet again Mom admitted that she had intentionally stopped taking her Lithium before the Running Bear episode, but couldn't remember why. I prayed that if only just for that one day, Mom's wig would stay on her head and her teeth in her mouth.

Bonnie and Jeanni were my only bridesmaids. I would have asked my sisters, but, as with my brothers, I just couldn't see them as part of a traditional wedding party. Since Mom hadn't been able to find a mother-of-the-bride dress she liked, I'd lent her a bridesmaid dress I'd worn in Jeanni's wedding a couple of years before. Though it was jarring to see her in such a young style, it seemed to make her happy. If she stayed happy, maybe she'd stay sane—at least until after my wedding.

In 1977, elaborate wedding dresses weren't cool, so I'd gone to an outlet in The City and bought a Victorian number for $12. Once again, Pat's good taste would have come in handy.

Gauzy, with long sleeves and high neck, the dress looked more like a nightgown than a wedding gown. Not $12 well spent, after all.

Dad stood next to Mom in rust tuxedo and ruffled peach shirt. He patted her shoulder. "Barb, you be good now."

"Daddy, my baby's getting married. I can't help it if I cry!" She dabbed her eyes again and blew her nose. Dad squeezed her hand, and their eyes met. They both smiled.

Someone tapped on the door, a signal that it was time to begin. I walked to the door, heart pounding. Mom took my face in her hands. "My baby girl." Her eyes were wet but calm. I drew her in, smelling her familiar fragrance, and held on tight. "I love you, Mom."

The Bach fugue that I had chosen as my wedding march began to play and Dean came to walk Mom to her seat in the front row. I took Dad's arm, and we walked up the aisle. My heart was full: all of the people I loved in one room! Better yet, I'd finally gotten contacts: I could see them! Auntie Sissy, looking tiny beside my tall cousins, grinned and waved from where she sat next to Uncle Jim, who had a portfolio next to him in the pew. Were there 45s inside his portfolio to play at the reception? Vera Dickie straightened her shoulders and gave a thumb's up. Joan, looking like Lauren Bacall in silk shirt and trousers as she sat next to a ponytailed Dan, smiled at me indulgently. Glenn sitting next to Nana, raised his eyebrows and opened his mouth in a silent scream of joy. Pat, detailed to cut Chief Running Bear off at the pass if necessary, held Mom's hand. I looked down the pew. Where was Sue? Dad walked me to Paul at the altar, gave me a kiss, and sat down next to Mom.

Paul squeezed my hand, and we gazed into each other's eyes. *Pull me in.* A guitarist sang, "You Are the Sunshine of My Life." Although Paul had chosen the song, the words rang true for both of us. When we kissed and were pronounced man and wife, my family led the cheers.

Paul and I marched jubilantly down the aisle and out the chapel door. At the curb, standing next to a vintage Rolls Royce in chauffer attire, was my sister Sue. I shrieked. When she threw open the back door with a flourish Paul and I, ducking a torrent of birdseed, climbed in. Sue smiled an all-your-teeth Cheshire cat smile as her eyes met mine in the rearview mirror. "I wanted my little sister to leave her wedding in style."

Chapter 17

❦

The Last Supper

18 Months Later

I rolled over onto my stomach on the lounge, adjusted my bikini, and covered my head with a towel. The sound of children playing in the pool grew quieter. Maybe getting my real estate license hadn't been such a bad idea: here I was on a Friday afternoon relaxing by the pool feeling the warm sun beat down on my thighs.

The year before, I'd decided to put off getting my master's degree and get my real estate license. I needed a break from school and could use the money I made toward a graduate degree. Or so I told myself. I was living in a condominium in the suburbs selling split-level ranch houses and had created nothing. Meanwhile my brothers and sisters were expressing themselves in all sorts of arenas: Glenn was a teacher, Pat had begun talking about moving to New York City where an exciting new art scene was taking shape; Sue was exploring options in the dance world; and Joan had a popular graphic design business. I told myself there was still time. I was only twenty-four.

A lilting laugh drifted through the rod iron fence. I pulled the towel off my head to see a familiar pair of suede Birkenstocks. "Joan!" I ran to the gate. It had been months since I'd seen her. She was arriving for a family Easter celebration.

Joan could have stayed at my parents' apartment in Castro Valley, or in The City with Pat or Glenn, but she'd chosen to stay with me. I chose to regard it as a validation: she—and so by extension, all my siblings—loved me no matter where I lived and what I was doing.

The two of us whipped up a batch of chocolate chip cookie dough, and I set it down on the new glass-topped coffee table in the living room. Joan crossed her legs yogi style on my new brown velour couch: she and Dan had gotten into transcendental meditation. With our friends, I was proud of the room's décor. With Joan, I felt ashamed. I no longer had my own style. I'd sold out and gone suburban.

"So Sue isn't coming up this weekend?" Joan searched the bowl of dough for a hefty clump and de-chipped it.

"No, she's teaching a dance class," I said. I scooped up the chips she'd left behind and tossed them in my mouth.

"What a brat. She said she was going to try and come." Joan replied, pretending to be mad.

I walked over to the kitchen table and picked up a large manila envelope. "She sent this." I pulled out a drawing of a stick figure with rabbit ears and big feathery tail. Underneath it, Sue had labeled *Shake a Tail Feather Sue*. "She said to put this on her chair at Easter dinner." We laughed.

Joan repositioned her legs as she changed the subject. "Do you think you want kids?" she said unexpectedly. It was weird that we had never discussed it.

"Yeah, but not right away; I'd still like to live in The City …" I said wistfully. All my life San Francisco had been just across the water, its white skyline like a city in a dream. Yet I had still never lived there.

Joan jumped in before I could finish. "Well then, you should do it, Peg."

I shrugged. "It's gonna take a miracle to get Paul to move there."

Joan twirled some hair around her right index finger. "So have you had any more nice dreams about me?"

I'd had a terrible nightmare a few weeks before that Dan had called me to say that Joan had died. It had felt so real that I'd woken up crying. I'd called her early the next morning to make sure she was okay.

I winced. "I'm sorry. I must have freaked you out."

"Yep," Joan said sarcastically, "You know *just* how to start off a person's day."

"Sometimes dreams mean just the opposite. Maybe you'll get a huge new client?" I asked hopefully.

Her voice trailed off as she grabbed another chunk of dough. "Yeah … maybe."

* * *

I was nervous about having everyone at our condo for Easter dinner: I'd never entertained before. I scanned the grocery list to make sure I hadn't forgotten anything: ham, carrots, and lemon for the sautéed carrot recipe I'd found, rolls, butter, bourbon, 7-Up, and carrot cake from the supermarket bakery. Thank God Mom was making everyone's favorite potato and macaroni salads just in case everything else was awful.

I set all of the food on the kitchen counter buffet style and was pleased that everyone had a full plate when they sat.

Mom made the sign of the cross, and we all said grace.

"Oops, almost forgot!" I said, propping up Sue's stick figure drawing on the table to great laughter. Then I took out the seven sets of bunny ears Sue had cut from white construction paper and colored with crayon and read from the note inside, "Wear these with pride while you gnaw on your ham and potato salad. No thumping or twitching at the table." Each set of ears had a name. Jack Rabbit and Mother Rabbit were easy enough to figure out. We fought over the others. Pat grabbed "Bugs," Glenn was "Brer Rabbit," Joan was "Flopsy," and Paul picked "Peter Cottontail." I got stuck with "Hare Truman."

No one hesitated to put them on.

"How's the state of the union, Hare Truman?" Jack Rabbit asked grinning, his pink and white rabbit ears blending nicely with his balding head.

"Just hoppin' along," I responded. I was rusty at dinner banter.

"So Brer Rabbit, how's the teaching going?" Mother Rabbit asked, cutting into her ham.

"Great," Glenn's ears flopped forward as he buttered his roll, "Head Royce has me teaching English History. They don't want you teaching the subject you majored in: they want the material fresh in your mind. I've honed my skills at drawing graphic depictions of medieval battles on the blackboard. My eighth graders love it. I promised if they all got good scores on their final I'd draw them a really gory picture. So far, they've memorized everything from the Roman Conquest through the Magna Carta." I'd visited Glenn's classroom. A ceramic statue of Henry the VIII's wife Ann Boleyn, head in hand, stood at the front of his desk. Made by one of his students as a gift, the statue was a testament to Glenn's sick humor. Next to it were a painted box from Nepal and a small beveled glass pyramid. On the front of his desk was a large sign that read THINK.

"Sounds lovely, Brer Rabbit," Patrick said, his front teeth hanging over his bottom lip like Bugs Bunny, "As long as you don't depict a bunny massacre, I'm perfectly okay with it." He turned to Joan, his ears waving. "How about you, Flopsy?"

Joan's ears quivered as she shook her head. "I'm glad I'm not in his classroom. I think I'd be sick." She broke character. "So Pat, when do you move to New York?"

Pat laughed as he set his rabbit ears on the table. "I just can't have a serious conversation with these on." He fluffed his hair, which was becoming more sparse like Dad's, over the scar on his forehead. "Not soon enough. San Francisco's become depressing since Milk and Moscone were murdered. I've got to get out of there."

"Well, Atarick," Mother Rabbit jumped in, "you've always said you wanted to be an artist in New York. It's about time."

"To Bugs in New York!" we cheered, our ears fluttering.

Chapter 18

All Hands on Deck

June 27, 1979

I pulled the pastries out of the white bag and placed them on my prettiest platter. I checked the coffee—it was brewing nicely. My friend and neighbor, JoAnne, would be coming over in another thirty minutes for coffee. It was her birthday. When the phone rang I assumed it was her. "Hey, Birthday Girl!"

"Uh, Peg, it's me ... Dan."

"*Dan*! What a great surprise! What are *you* doing calling?

"Uh, no, Peg. Uh, shit ... okay, I want you to listen carefully. Get a pencil and paper: I want you to write down this number."

Dan was a great prankster: I'd heard this mock serious voice before. I wasn't falling for it, not this time. "Okay, Dan, but I'm on to you. What are you up to now?"

"First write down this number, 916-863-4412. You can call me there anytime over the next few days."

"Sure, Danny, got it. Okay, now what?" I asked, writing down the number but ready to crumple it up when he was done. I rolled my eyes and tapped the counter with my fingertips.

"Peg, this is the hardest thing I've ever had to do in my life and *Geezus* ... I just don't know how to do it, so I'm just going to tell you. Joan's dead."

I laughed. Joan must have told him about my dream. "Nice try, Danny."

But he wasn't laughing. My heart started to pound. "Danny, you're kidding, right?" The silence pulled at my feet like a strong undertow before a huge wave. "Danny!" I yelped into the phone. "Oh my God, Danny, you're not kidding, are you?" Everything around me blurred. I fell with a thud on the floor. I dug my fingers into my scalp, tucked my head in tight to my chest, and pulled my legs in.

Dan's voice called from the surface a million miles away "Peg, are you there?"

I pulled the base of the phone near, desperate for one last connection with my sister. "How did it happen?" I asked, my voice choking.

Danny drew an uneven breath. "I came home from work yesterday afternoon and found her." He stopped talking as he sobbed.

My body went cold.

"Her clothes were ripped off," he stopped again, "and there was blood everywhere. She was stabbed ... all over," there was a clunk as if he put the receiver down.

I squeezed my eyes shut and rocked back and forth on my knees. *No more, no more, no more.* But Dan got back on. "The phone cord was wrapped around her neck, Peg. She must have put up a hell of a fight," He sniffed and exhaled unevenly.

I dropped the phone and gripped my hands in prayer. I tried to imagine Joan's pain ... her horror at being attacked ... her fear

of dying. I rocked faster … *Please Dear God, give it all to me …*
I rolled onto the floor and sobbed. I imagined Danny entering
their house through the kitchen, seeing the trail of blood, and
finding Joan in their room on the floor, bloodied and strangled.

Suddenly, my body was still. No more Joan at Easter or
Christmas. No more talks. No more meandering rides. No more
sharing cookie dough. No lilting laughter … ever … ever again.

"Peg?" Dan asked anxiously.

"I'm here," I said, groggily. "Dan … how did Mom take it?"
I asked, the full force of reality hitting me now.

Danny was silent. My heart stopped.

"Peg, I'm sorry." He said quietly.

"You haven't told my family?"

"I can't do it. I need you to do it," he pleaded.

An image of Joan and Dan wrapped in each other's arms
shot through my head. Suddenly, I felt oddly protective of him.
"Okay," I said, gasping for air.

I dialed Paul's number at work.

"Berkeley Forge and Tool," the company's British secretary
answered cheerfully.

"Sheila, I need to talk to Paul," I replied in as businesslike a
voice as I could muster.

"Peggy? You sound dreadful. I'll get him right away," Sheila
said.

Paul picked up the phone. "What is it?"

I started to cry, but tried to talk. "It's … it's … Joan."

"What?" he asked. A huge hammer pounding steel nearby
made it difficult for him to hear.

"She's dead."

"Your roommate Joni died?"

"No, Joan … my sister … Joan's been murdered!"

"Stay there," he said calmly. "I'll be right there."

I put the phone back on the hook and picked it up again,
listening to the dial tone. Somewhere in the distance, a leaf
blower roared, and a dog barked at it. I dug nails into my palms.

Then I forced myself to dial Sue's number. I hadn't thought about what to say. Sue lived to dance at clubs late into the night. She was waitressing dinners. She'd most likely still be asleep.

"Hello?" she answered, her voice scratchy.

"Hey, Sue," I said quietly.

"Pegs?" she asked, the scratchiness stretching into a question.

"Sue I have the worst news in the world to tell you."

Her voice sat up straight. "Pegs. Is it Mom … is she okay?" Worrying about Mom's mental health was second nature to us all.

"It's Joan," I said wanting desperately to shove the words back in my mouth. "Joan's dead."

A scream caught in her throat. She wailed for what seemed forever. Suddenly, there was silence.

"Sue, don't hang up. Sue … do you hear me—please, please don't hang up. Sue … God, I am so sorry. Sue, I love you. Are you there?"

"I'm here," Sue said through a body shuddering sob. "Okay, tell me what happened."

I recounted what Dan had told me, and we cried together. She said she would call Pat, who was visiting friends in LA before moving to New York, and I would call Glenn.

"Sue? What about Mom?"

Sue was quiet for a moment. "I think we all need to be there to tell Mom and Dad."

"You're right." I was relieved that she was taking the lead.

"Peg …?" Sue asked softly. "I love you too … thanks for being the one to tell me," she said.

* * *

When Glenn met me outside his school and heard me out, he patted my shoulder and hurried toward the street. For a moment,

I thought he was going to go talk to Paul, who was waiting in the car. Instead he walked across the street, opened the door of his weathered orange Datsun 240Z, and sped away.

* * *

Paul and I waited at the airport gate for Pat and Sue who were flying in from LA. Pat, eyes red and wide open like in Munch's painting, *The Scream*, walked in front of Sue, who leaned into a tall, muscular blonde woman as she moved. *That must be Sue's new girlfriend. Dee. She can use someone big and strong right now.*

Paul and Dee took a few steps back as Pat, Sue, and I huddled in the middle of the airport breezeway, quaking with sobs. People were silent as they walked past and stared.

Glenn was parked across the street from Mom and Dad's apartment complex when we drove up. For the first time in memory we did not smile upon seeing each other. Patrick took my hand, and Glenn Sue's, as we walked toward Mom and Dad's unit. Worn blue carpet ran alongside white walls smudged with nicks and handprints, evidence of renters moving in and out. Patrick knocked: the plywood door sounded hollow. Footsteps approached. We took a collective deep breath.

Mom smiled broadly when she opened the door, "What a nice surprise! Daddy, all our babies are here!" She scanned us as we walked in. There were only four. Her eyes darkened. "*Where's Joanie?*"

Daddy came up beside Mom.

Without hesitating, Glenn spouted, "Joan fell and broke her neck. She died right away, Mom." Sue, Pat, and I stared at him in disbelief.

Daddy stepped backward and slumped against the dining room table as though he'd been shot. Mom found her way to the burnt orange chair they'd shoved into the corner of the small living room. We each hugged Dad before sitting around Mom:

an attempt to form a barrier to keep her from tumbling into the abyss. Mom wrapped her arms around herself and rocked back and forth, tears flowing.

"Maybe it's for the best. Our Joanie could have died in childbirth. This way it was quick and painless." Mom said, her logic bizarre in her grief.

Sue grabbed Glenn by the arm and dragged him into the bathroom.

Dad pushed himself off the dining room table and shuffled into the kitchen. I heard the sounds of him making coffee. The pot clinked against the sink as he put it on the counter.

I listened outside the bathroom to what Glenn and Sue were saying.

"What the hell were you thinking?" Sue hissed.

"We should tell them that their daughter was stabbed, raped, and strangled to death?" Glenn asked sarcastically.

"They're going to find out anyway!"

Pat tapped on the door and walked in. I followed him in and closed the door.

"I agree with Sue," Patrick said.

Glenn stormed out the front door.

"Mom and Dad," Patrick said in the living room, "we need to talk with you." Patrick took Mom's hand. Sue took her other hand. Dad sat down on the couch. I put my hand on his back as though I could prop up a tree about to be sawn through.

"Joan didn't fall and break her neck," Pat said, his voice breaking, "she was murdered. Someone broke in after Dan left for work yesterday. I won't go into the details." He stopped. "But it was violent. Dan's been dealing drugs. We think it may have been some sort of retribution."

Mom's silence was terrible. She was white-faced and trembling. Dad leaned forward and grabbed the top of his head with both hands. I rubbed his back hopelessly.

To our amazement, as the day wore on, Mom found strength. She called her sisters, Noreen and Marie, and Dad's siblings, Betty,

Sis, and Jim. Each time she said "We lost our Joanie yesterday," her voice broke, and she'd need a tissue, but her grief was normal. By the end of the day, she had found a chapel for Joan's Rosary and a cemetery for her body.

The six of us read quietly in the small living room that night, each of us trying to escape to anywhere we could, if only for an hour or two. Cigarette smoke filled the room. We slept where we found ourselves when Dad turned off the lights. I lay on the floor of the living room with Joan's old chenille bedspread wrapped round me. Sue's head poked out from a sleeping bag on the couch, and Patrick lay crosswise at my feet on the floor. Glenn had ended up sleeping in the guest bedroom.

It was still dark outside when Dad shuffled into the kitchen. By the glow of the bulb above the stove, he stared at the front door. A minute later, he peered into the guest room and then wandered into the living room and looked around at us. Was he looking for Joan? He closed his eyes and bowed his head, then went to the dining room table, pulled out a chair, and slumped down heavily.

A sharp pain gripped my stomach. *Joan is gone.* Her bloody body in her yellow robe filled my head. *No!* Joan's voice screamed in my head as a dark figure wrapped the cord around her neck. "Her clothes were ripped off." The shadowy figure held her down. I pulled the covers over my head. Oh, my God … *Joan was still alive when he strangled her.* My body convulsed with muffled sobs.

A hand touched my head through the blanket. "Peg?" Patrick whispered.

"Yeah?"

He gently pulled the blanket off my head, crouched down next to me, and kissed me on the forehead. "Ah Peggle," he said, wiping away his own tears, "The pain is unbelievable, isn't it?"

I nodded and wiped my eyes. He walked into the bathroom. I sat up.

"Hey, sport," Dad said with a tight smile from the kitchen.

"Hey, Daddy." I went over to give him a hug.

He hugged me back tightly. "Well, since we're up, I'll make some coffee." He struggled to push himself up from the table. "Your mother and I haven't slept at all."

I walked into their bedroom. Mom sat propped up against her headboard, smoking. The ashtray was full of butts. She held out her arms, and I ran to her embrace.

After we had drenched each other's shoulders. she said, "She's one of God's angels now, honey. Knowing our Joanie, she'll be bossing them around in no time."

* * *

Joan's old boyfriend Larry and Sue's ex-partner Anita, both a part of our extended family circle, joined the cheerless convoy to Susanville for Joan's funeral.

Dan's parents, who'd loved Joan like a daughter, stood behind Dan as we drove up to the motel outside of Susanville. He obviously needed their support. Behind his wire rim glasses, his eyes held a freakish surprise as though he'd stuck his finger in a light socket. His hug, once strong, was limp. Like a fallen angel, Dan had lost both power and beauty.

Pat hugged Dan, his jaw tight. If Dan hadn't looked so helpless, I'll bet Pat would have punched him. Instead, Pat walked over to the bench in front of the lobby, sat down, and lit a cigarette. He blamed himself, he said. If he hadn't introduced Dan to Joan, Joan would still be alive.

Mom and Dad knew that Joan wouldn't have wanted a traditional Rosary, so instead they invited people to simply sit and pray in the chapel while Joan's casket was present. The mortician denied their request for an open casket, saying that Joan's body was beyond repair. We would never see our Joanie again.

Later that night, we siblings went down to the police station. The clues were minimal: no fingerprints to speak of, some gold missing from a hole punched in the living room wall, some drugs obviously removed from the house prior to the call to the police, no barking dog. Obviously, Joan's dog knew who it was. Two glasses of orange juice had been poured on the counter after Dan had left, but Joan was allergic to orange juice. If Joan's hair was down, did it mean she had been waiting for whoever ended up killing her? Was she seeing anyone? Did she have any enemies? Did we know any of Dan's friends … his enemies? Would Dan, the police persisted, have done this to her?

Did we want to see the photos? The images in my mind were horrid enough. I didn't need real photos burned into my memory. Sue saw them, but as I had suspected, they only made her feel worse.

"We believe that your sister was killed in retaliation for a bad drug deal that her husband made," the middle-aged police sergeant leading the investigation said, "but her husband isn't sharing information about who he's dealt with. We've known he's been selling drugs for years, but we've never been able to catch him at it."

"That bastard!" Sue yelled.

"Dan's agreed to take a lie detector test next week," the sergeant continued, "but we'll need him to give us his contacts if we're going to solve this case."

As we pushed out our chairs around the table, the sergeant stood and cleared his throat. "In all my twenty-five years in the force, I've never seen anything like this. My heart goes out to your family. We will work with the FBI and follow up on every clue until we figure out who's done this terrible thing."

Danny passed his lie detector test. Though he provided information on his drug contacts, they led nowhere. Having slashed a gaping hole in our family circle, Joan's killer got away clean.

* * *

Patrick, Paul, and I were the last of our family to enter the chapel the next day. Dan sat in the second row from the altar, his legs crossed yogi style on the pew. His family and some of his and Joan's friends sat behind them. Dee and Sue and Anita and Larry sat next to Glenn, Mom, and Dad. I kneeled at their pew, making the sign of the cross as I stared at the yellow casket Mom had chosen.

"Take care of Daddy, Peg," Pat whispered as he walked by on his way to kneel down in front of the casket. For the first time in my life, I couldn't bring myself to follow him. That body in the box wasn't Joan. As far as I was concerned, Joan was walking around among us. Paul followed me as I scooted in beside Dad, who was bent forward with his hand on his forehead. I'd been trained well to take care of Mom. In twenty-five years, no one had ever trained me to take care of Dad.

I took Dad's hand. His breathing trembled and his shoulders began to shake as his hand gripped mine. Finally, his tears came. I wrapped my arm tightly around his shoulder. All of a sudden, he was standing. Facing the cross, he called out "*Why our Joanie?*" Everyone turned to stare. Dad gripped the back of the pew before repeating once again, louder, "WHY OUR JOANIE?" His voice echoed off the ceiling. The one and only time in his whole life he'd ever protested, and no one answered.

"Jack, honey," Mom said, their roles reversed as she softly took his hand, "Sit down."

As he sat, I wrapped my arms around him. "She's okay now, Daddy. I know she's okay," I uttered inanely.

That afternoon, we created a large circle with Joan and Dan's friends in a field filled with wildflowers to mourn our dead sister and daughter. Many people stepped into the circle to talk about Joan, but my family's overwhelming sorrow rendered us speechless.

That evening, a large group of us shared a surreal family-style Italian dinner with many bottles of wine. Dad imbibed heavily.

When, after dinner, Daddy decided to go for a walk, Paul and I thought it best that we join him.

We struggled to hold him up as he stumbled over rocks and holes in the field next to the restaurant. He was like a paratrooper who, having jumped into enemy territory, fights to disengage himself from his tangled chute. As he staggered, he belted out the words to an old army drinking song: "*Ooooohhhh this is number three and her hand is on my knee, roll me over lay me down and do it again—roll me over in the clover, roll me over, lay me down and do it again ...*"

Part III

Crash or Fly

1981–1992

Chapter 19

❦

The Eternal Dance

July, 1981

Stand up in a clear blue morning until you see what can be. Alone in a cold day dawning, are you still free? Can you be? Steve Winwood blared from the radio of my BMW as I navigated the twisting canyon road that wound from my house in San Ramon to my parents' apartment in Castro Valley. Calves, born that spring, lay next to their mothers on the golden hills. I'd taken a leave from selling real estate and was bored. I needed to get out and go somewhere, anywhere.

Mom opened her apartment door just before I had the chance to knock. We laughed as she tried to wrap her arms around me. One week past my due date, I felt like what poet Sylvia Plath had called a watermelon strolling on two tendrils.

"God, I'll be happy when I finally have this baby," I said, leaning back on the green velveteen couch that Glenn had bought at a thrift store to replace my parents' worn white sofa.

"Egetha, you're just like me," Mom sat down in her green leather chair, one of the few things she'd inherited from her parents' estate. "All of my babies were born late." She took a deep puff from her cigarette and exhaled.

Any resemblance to Mom's childbirth experience made me uneasy: I'd avoided going crazy when I was nineteen, but would I have a breakdown like Mom did again after her first baby? If I did, would Paul stick around? I wiped the sweat from my upper lip. Paul had been a doting expectant father, making sure I got enough rest and running out to pick up Mexican food, the only thing I ever seemed to crave. He'd said he wasn't sure if he was ready to be a father, but I knew he was just nervous. I smiled. Like my Dad, Paul would be an anchor, providing love and security for me and our baby, no matter what.

It had been four years since Mom's last breakdown just before my wedding. Finally comfortable talking about her mental illness, Mom was now able to recognize its manifestations and called the doctor if her medication needed adjusting.

A warm breeze floated in the open sliding door that led to my parents' patio. Through the rod-iron fence, a young mother sat on the top stair of the shallow end of the pool dipping her baby's feet in the water. Up and down and up and down—with each dip came another tiny surprised giggle. Soon, I would be dipping my own baby's feet in the water. Was I ready?

Suddenly very warm, I gathered my hair together and held it in a ponytail atop my head. I had hoped to have the baby on June 26, the second anniversary of Joan's death. Shortly after Joan died, a psychic told us that our sister wanted to be reborn back into our family. We didn't dare tell Mom and Dad. But would we be able to tell if the baby was Joan? Would it have her bright blue eyes and fine blonde hair?

"Stop it, Peg ... Don't put all of that on the poor baby. You will love it no matter who it is," Joan's voice took on a bossy tone in my mind. Ever since she died, Joan was my Dear Abby, on call day or night, answering my questions with wit, wisdom, and, if I was lucky, a lilting laugh. *But what if I don't love the baby?* The question had haunted me for weeks. On this one, Joan was silent.

My father emerged from the bathroom. "There he is!" I said. I struggled to push myself off the couch to give him a hug, but the baby pushed into my rib cage, squeezing the air from my lungs. I fell back down. Dad came over and kissed me on the head. "Don't get up, Peg. It's too painful to watch."

He went in to the kitchen, poured himself a cup of coffee, and came back to sit down on the burnt orange chair across from me. His eyes were red: Had he been crying? Up until Joan's death, Daddy was stoic. Now, the slightest tender scene made him teary-eyed. Mom said he often wandered around the apartment looking for things but never seemed to find them. Somehow, she said, he always ended up in the bathroom.

"Mom?" I asked quietly.

"What honey?" Mom replied tapping her cigarette into the ashtray at her side.

"What if I don't love the baby?" I asked nervously. "I mean ... what if I have it and decide I don't really want it?"

Mom started to giggle. But I wasn't trying to be funny.

"Mom, I'm serious. I'm kinda scared about that."

But Mom kept laughing. Tears formed in her eyes. She doubled over and grabbed a tissue. "Daddy," she called into the kitchen. Dad walked the few steps into the living room. "Peg wants to know what to do if she doesn't like the baby."

For the first time since Joan died, my father threw back his head and laughed heartily. "Well, if worse comes to worse, we can sell it at a garage sale. They'll get you a good price for it." The thought of not adoring your child from the moment it was born was completely alien to them.

"Well, Daddy, are you ready to head over to Longs?" Mom asked.

"In a minute," Dad replied. "Let me finish my coffee."

If their car had been a horse, it would have automatically carried them to the Longs Drugs situated less than two miles from their apartment. *Something* was always needed: an extra can of coffee on sale, clams for dip, or a few towels for one of us kids. One day I counted fourteen cans of mushroom soup all lined up on the shelf of their cupboard. Filling their cupboards seemed to help fill the giant void in their hearts.

Glenn and I had made a point of spending more time with Mom and Dad these past two years. Sue, who'd grown tired of eking out a living teaching dance, opened a hair salon in Santa Rosa with her partner, Dee. "Doing hair," she said, "is like a dance performance: you know right away whether your creation is a hit or a flop." Pat was living in New York designing fabrics for Joe Boxer and printing rare books with his partner, Tom. Since Joan's death, neither Pat nor Sue came home often.

It had been a difficult two years for Mom and Dad. Six months after Joan's death, Nana died. As long as I could remember, Mom had tried to win her mother's love. It finally came when Nana entered a rest home and Mom took a job there to care for her. The brief closeness they shared during those final days made Nana's passing more difficult. Despite her heartbreaking losses, my mother had grown stronger. Dad, on the other hand, had not: our family's anchor had begun drifting away.

Money got tighter as their rent and other expenses increased. Dad's benefits included health insurance and cost of living increases. But there were always unforeseen bills to be paid. Though each of us kids offered my parents money, they rarely took it. Mom hoped to inherit some money from her mother. Finally, she and Dad would be able to pay off their bills and stash a little money away.

It was not to be. When Mom's brother Jack died suddenly of a heart attack four years before, Nana appointed her eldest daughter Noreen as the executor of her estate. A few months later, Jack's children received a letter from Nana's attorney stating that they would no longer be beneficiaries of her estate. Still reeling from their father's sudden death, my cousins never challenged the letter or Nana's uncharacteristic change of heart.

When Nana moved into the rest home, she asked Noreen to sell her duplex. The proceeds were to be combined with her stocks and bank accounts and split equally among her children and their heirs. A few months before she died, Nana confided to her daughter Marie's husband, Joe, that she was concerned about her account. The following day, the banker explained that there had been several withdrawals over the past two years, many for sizeable amounts. He said they hadn't seen much of Nana at the bank, only my Aunt Noreen and her son Michael. At one time, Michael had been an up-and-coming football star playing for Notre Dame. After graduating, he married and had two daughters. But his successes didn't follow him off the field. Over the following years, he bounced from job to job. He and his wife divorced. He remarried and had four more children and found it even harder to make ends meet.

Nana had been duped into signing all of her stocks over to Noreen, who, in turn, signed them over to my cousin Michael. There was a good reason why, as a child, the thought of Aunt Noreen had always conjured up a swirling tornado in my mind.

The day after Nana died, Aunt Noreen invited Mom and Dad and Marie and Joe over for a dinner of pink beans and ham hocks. Noreen, Mom related later, had broken down in a dramatic flood of tears as she explained that between the cost of Nana's stay at the rest home and frequent doctor visits, all of her money and stock investments had been spent.

Mom imitated Aunt Noreen's performance for me: "And the worst part is," she said, pretending to cry dramatically into a tissue, "I don't even have the money to help you pay for Mother's funeral." My parents and Aunt Marie and Uncle Joe sued Aunt Noreen and Michael, the bank, and the stock brokerage company, but to no avail. Their portion of Nana's inheritance, about $60,000, had already been spent.

Dad walked into the kitchen, rinsed his coffee cup, and put it in the sink.

* * *

July 2, 1981

I looked into the eyes of the baby Paul and I had decided to name Shane. I saw Joan, but I also saw Glenn, Pat, and Sue. I saw Paul and Mom and Dad. I even saw myself. But this was someone new, regardless of who they used to be. And this would be a new life, a life in which this baby would learn to love and *be*. I held him tight. How could a person fall in love so quickly? *I'll take care of you, I promise. I'll always love you, and I will never ever consider selling you at a garage sale.*

I'd forgotten to call Mom and Dad! Their phone barely had the chance to ring before Mom picked up. "Hello?" she answered breathlessly.

"Hey, Mom, it's me," I said, trying to sound nonchalant. "Guess what?" I continued, trying hard not to cry, "I just had a baby boy!"

There was silence on the other end of the phone. I heard Mom take a big gulp of air like you do when you're starting to cry but trying to talk. I imagined her holding the receiver tightly in her hand as she squeezed her eyes shut with joy.

Finally she said, "Honey, that's just the best news I think I've ever heard," and started to cry.

Daddy took the phone. As I gave him all the details, I imagined him grinning from ear to ear.

Once Mom composed herself, she took back the phone and said quickly, "We'll be right there."

I laughed, holding on to the receiver after I was done, marveling at how, in the end, things were really very simple: death and life and sorrow and joy circling round and round in an eternal dance of *being*.

May, 1984

We'd had a party to celebrate my parents' thirty-seventh wedding anniversary at my house in San Ramon. Though Mom complained of bloating from her new medication, she and Dad danced happily on our deck as a host of friends and family looked on. Sue helped clean up before taking off to cut a client's hair. Glenn was leaving the next day to stay with friends on Fire Island in New York. I'd heard it was a gay Mecca, swarming with handsome men. "Have fun Glenn. Try to get a little sleep on your vacation,"

I smiled but a pang of worry shot through my stomach. AIDS was running rampant through the gay community. I hugged him tight. "Be careful."

"Of course I will," he smiled, but shook his head mischievously.

I had agreed to drive Pat to the airport later that evening. I rapped on the partially opened bedroom door.

"Hey, Peg, great party," he said, zipping his duffle bag.

Pat had always been more monogamous than Glenn. Should I be worried about him, too?

Shane's carefree giggle came from the backyard as Paul tackled and tickled him.

"Shane's really great, Peg," Pat said as he put his arm around my shoulders, "Who knew our little Peggle would make such a wonderful mother?"

Chapter 20

❦

Sidestroking the Tsunami

June, 1984

"Your mother's in the pool," Dad's voice crackled over the phone. It was 10:30 p.m. Although the apartment pool closed at 10:00, her still being in the pool in and of itself was not alarming. Was Mom just craving some exercise? "She doesn't have any clothes on," Daddy added, almost apologetically.

"Bathing suit?" I asked hopefully.

"No, no suit. And she's singing. I think you better come now. People are coming out." He hung up the phone.

It had been seven years since Mom's last incident. My reaction time had slowed. I grabbed an overnight bag and crammed in some clothes. *The bloating must have made her stop taking her pills.*

"I'll call you when I know what's going on," I said to Paul, giving him a quick peck before glancing into Shane's room: fast asleep. I ran downstairs and grabbed my keys. I arrived at Mom and Dad's apartment in ten minutes.

As I approached, Mom's unmistakably rich voice warbled "Moon River." People were standing on their balconies gawking down at the pool. Back and forth and back and forth she swam. Daddy stood next to the pool, shivering in his swimsuit. When he saw me he shook his head and made a tight smile.

I opened the gate to the pool. "Hi, Daddy," I said, giving him a hug.

"Hi, sport," he said grimly. "She says she's not ready to get out yet."

"Have you called the doctor?"

"Yes," he said. His lips crumpled. "He said I should call the police. They should be here soon."

Mom stopped singing. "Hi, Peg!" she called as though I'd stopped by for a visit.

Everyone's attention turned my way. "Hi, Mom," I said, loving her, but totally exasperated. "How about you get out of the pool now?"

"How about you get naked and join her in the pool?" some smart ass called down from one of the apartment balconies. I ignored him.

The police car pulled up next to the rod-iron fence. Two officers got out.

One of the officers addressed the crowd, "Okay, folks, the show's over." A few people stayed on their balconies.

The other policeman walked around the pool to the stairs. "Mrs. Kennedy, I'd appreciate it if you would get out now."

"But officer, I love having the pool all to myself," Mom replied coyly, flapping her hands in the water.

"Next time, wear your suit and come out as soon as the pool closes," he said as though speaking to a juvenile delinquent.

Never one to defy authority for long, Mom walked to the stairs and stepped out. The officer looked away as he gave her a towel. Mom dried off and handed it back to him. Subdued laughter came from one of the balconies.

The officer was unfazed as he handed the towel back. "Please wrap this around yourself." She did as she was told and followed Dad, who opened their patio gate. I followed the police inside the apartment. Someone knocked, and I opened the door. Two ambulance attendants were in the hall with a gurney. I tensed up: Mom had always fought being put on a gurney. But in the 1970s new laws put stringent limitations on committing mentally ill people involuntarily. Things were different now; she had to go willingly. The officers were there to make sure she did.

"Mrs. Kennedy ..." one of the officers said.

"You can call me Barbara," Mom said pleasantly, her arms wrapping her towel across her chest like a pinup girl.

"Barbara," he said hesitantly, "you might be a little warmer if you put some clothes on."

Mom's clothes were right where she had taken them off on the dining room table. She dropped the towel, slipped on her pants and top, and looked at the office, tilting her head like a curious puppy.

"Barbara, would you like to lie on the gurney?" He pointed out to the hallway.

"No, I don't think so," she shook her head.

"Well then, you'll need to come with us," he replied firmly. Would you mind doing that?"

"I can do that," she said with a benign smile.

The officers spoke quietly with the two ambulance guys. Getting antsy, Mom put her arms out, "Shall we go, boys?"

When she walked out on her own, the ambulance drove off.

Dad and I watched the officer help Mom into the backseat of the police car. Mom waved as the door closed.

When they turned out the driveway, Dad smiled cheerlessly and scratched his ear. He was only fifty-eight, but his blue eyes no longer sparkled. Still in his bathing suit, he had slumped shoulders. His arms had lost their muscle tone. His skin was sallow, and he winded easily. He looked more seventy-eight than fifty-eight. If he had tried to save Mom from drowning, she might have taken him down with her.

How many times had he watched an ambulance or police car drive away with Mom? Yet here he stood, willing to go through it again.

Paul would do the same for me. And I … would I be willing to do it for Paul? Lately it seemed as if we were fighting all the time. I often felt empty inside. Sometimes I thought of leaving, but then things would get better. What if there came a day when they didn't?

"Daddy …" I hesitated. Thrown off by his earnest stare, I stopped. His lips were cracked, his face weathered.

I took a breath and started again. "Over the years have you ever thought about … leaving Mom? I mean … you've put up with so much."

He squinted. It was plain the thought had never crossed his mind.

He shook his head. "She's my wife."

Chapter 21

❦

White Go-Go Boots

September, 1984

"Here you go again, overcommitting yourself! Why do you have to sign up for everything?" Paul asked with exasperation.

Oh my God, we were back in high school! I scraped the spaghetti from our dinner plates into the sink irritably. I hated the greasy residue the sauce left behind. My life had become an endlessly boring repetition of spaghetti dinners and television.

I always enjoyed putting on dances in high school. So when I was asked to join a group of San Ramon women to plan a black-tie fund-raiser for the following May, I eagerly agreed. That night, as Paul sat on the couch watching television, I told him I'd be going to fund-raiser planning meetings each week. He scowled, which made me angry. I loaded the dishwasher and slammed it shut. "You know, you do the things that you like to do. You run a few times each ..."

"I only run for thirty minutes," he interrupted. "You'll be gone for two or three hours at a time."

I walked into the laundry room, pulled a load of clothes out of the dryer, and started to fold them. He followed me.

"Can you stop what you're doing for one lousy minute so we can talk about this?"

"I think we need counseling—someone that can help us to figure this out," I said, folding one of Shane's small shirts.

"You're the one with the problem, not me," he said. "I don't need counseling."

"Fine," I said, picking up the folded clothes. "It's *my* problem. Maybe *I'll* go see someone." I brushed past him and headed up the stairs.

* * *

A few months later

I rushed through preparing a list of houses to show my clients that afternoon so that I could begin the work I had discovered I really enjoyed: finding corporate sponsors for our black-tie fundraiser. I was thrilled when a local hospital listened to my pitch and agreed to make a $1,000 donation. Later that day when a buyer made an offer, and it was accepted, I found it made no impact on me at all, though I would once have been ecstatic.

Our black-tie event needed special lighting, so the committee contacted several lighting companies. A few weeks later, George, a dark-haired young man from a San Francisco–based lighting company dressed in a hip black suit and red tie, breezed through a slideshow of events his company had done: San Francisco's Black and White Ball, an opening for the San Francisco Opera, a party for the cast of the second *Indiana Jones* movie. I was impressed.

"I think you ladies should aim at blowing everyone away," he said. "We've got a laser show; a huge mirrored ball, and I can recommend an incredible band. Of course, if you prefer, we could keep it boring so that everyone will leave by 9:00 and you'll all be able to go home and go to bed. Isn't that what you do out here in San Ramote?"

We all laughed at the well-worn dig. He was obviously gay—he was too funny and creative to be straight. "We're not as remote as you think," I laughed.

His eyes flashed. "Well, that's really good to hear," he said, biting his lip as he looked directly at me. The sarcasm was gone from his voice. Was he flirting with me? I shrugged it off. He was gay. And yet …

Our group agreed to hire him. As he packed up his slideshow, he turned to me. "Are you from here?"

"Kind of," I replied with a smile. "I grew up in the Bay Area."

"You seem different from the others," he said, focusing his full attention on me. I was flattered to be singled out. "Next time I'm out here, would you like to have coffee?"

"Sure!" I said without hesitation. Gay men reminded me of my brothers.

We met a couple of weeks later at a local coffee shop, where I discovered that he'd gone to UC Santa Cruz like Pat; was just a year older than I; and lived in a flat in The Castro—definitely gay! Though his sarcasm was biting, he was, like my brothers, hilariously funny. I'd forgotten what it felt like to really laugh. When we shook hands good-bye, I wondered if he had a partner: if so, was he as entertaining as George?

That next Sunday, Paul went motocross racing in Placerville early in the morning while Shane and I were still asleep. That afternoon, he called from a hospital in Sacramento with a broken leg.

I took Shane to Mom and Dad's before leaving for Sacramento. After her naked swim in the pool, Mom was hospitalized in a local psychiatric hospital for a few days. When she was released, she agreed to start getting Lithium shots every two weeks. They didn't make her bloated and regulated her illness well. Most importantly, we knew that she was getting her medicine.

When I arrived at the hospital, Paul was in surgery, having a pin put in his leg. Although he was on heavy medication the next day when I drove him home in our Jeep, every bump in the road made him writhe in pain. But nothing made him more miserable than the thought of losing his mobility for two whole months.

We bought Paul's brother's van so that Paul could sit comfortably while I drove. During his convalescence, Paul's mood was often foul. We argued incessantly. When I decided to attend a black-tie fund-raiser meeting again two weeks after he got home, Paul threw his crutch at me as I walked out the door.

I kept waiting for things to get better between us, but they didn't. Being for the most part immobile, Paul seemed to want to control my every movement. I, on the other hand, had begun to realize that my knack for developing corporate sponsorship might lead me to a more exciting career than real estate. The fledgling event sponsorship industry was growing as corporations looked to ways outside traditional advertising to get their message across. Here, finally, was a career in which I could combine both my creativity and sales abilities. A success with this fund-raiser could be my entrée into this compelling new world. Over the next two months, I contacted countless numbers of potential sponsors.

* * *

May, 1985

Though Paul was still on crutches the evening of the fund-raiser, his mood had improved because he was due to get his cast off. The room was alive with massive Mardi Gras masks, laser lights, and people milling in fashionable long gowns and tuxedos around the silent auction tables. Colorful helium balloons covered the ceiling. After dinner, the lights dimmed and the disco ball spun as the band played Motown. I loved this music! Since Paul couldn't dance, I danced with the other volunteers, who were jubilant that everything had gone off so well. I was euphoric: I'd far exceeded the committee's expectations for corporate sponsorship.

"Come dance with me!" I chided George as he talked with the DJ. He'd been avoiding me all night. As I took his hand, he glanced over at Paul.

"He doesn't care!" I said. *Why would he care, when you're gay?*

He had great rhythm—*definitely gay*. The song segued into another and we kept dancing.

When I returned to the table, Paul glared at me. "Who was that?"

"Oh, that was the special effects guy, George. Don't worry, he's gay."

Exhausted after the event that night, we volunteers all agreed to meet at noon the next day to clean up.

In the daylight, the building that had been so lively the night before looked drab. I walked up the stairs to the space where we'd had our event. *Where is everyone?* The floor was sprinkled with confetti, and the colorful helium balloons now hovered within reach. The caterer had cleared all of the dishes and glassware the night before, but drink napkins were scattered where the bar had been. A few unclaimed auction items sat off in a corner.

"The brooms are over here," a man's voice said. I turned. Across the room, George was dismantling the laser lighting system. Dressed in fatigue pants and T-shirt, he looked much more masculine than in a suit or tux.

"Hi!" I said, pleased to see him. "Where is everyone?"

"No one's here yet. I figured that you would come to help clean up," he said smiling. "I'm glad you're here." His deep blue eyes fixed on mine.

Then, just like that, with spent helium balloons eddying around our feet, he kissed me. I didn't move away. The kiss grew more passionate. He reached for the zipper of my blue jean jumpsuit and started to unzip it. I stepped back and took a deep breath.

"I thought you were gay!" I said, still reeling.

He laughed. "Why, because I live in San Francisco?" He shook his head and smiled. "Nope, definitely straight, and definitely attracted to you."

"I'm married," I blurted out.

"I know." He took my hand. "That's why I never said anything before. But last night as we danced I thought I saw something more in the way you looked at me." He kissed my hand.

I pulled it away and rubbed my face as though trying to wash the desire away. Voices downstairs ... I sighed loudly. "Let me think about this," I said, my heart still pounding.

The other volunteers came in and started cleaning up. I grabbed a broom. *Holy shit!* I swept the floor, not wanting to make conversation with anyone so I could think. I hadn't felt so energized in years.

* * *

Paul's cast came off the following week. As his mood improved, our arguments decreased. George hadn't called.

Now that he was mobile again, Paul wanted to drive something sporty. As we sat in the Porsche sales office, my shoulders tightened. The mass of material things in my life was burying who I really was. The real me had been happy driving my old green Volkswagen.

I went alone to marriage counseling. "My husband thinks I'm unhappy with him, but I'm not. I'm unhappy with me!" I told her.

A few visits later the marriage counselor asked: "Have you ever considered a trial separation?"

"I made a vow. I can't break it." Dad's face popped into my head.

"You're not doing your husband any favors by staying. Maybe you should take a break from each other."

I cried again, this time, from relief. No one had ever said it was okay to leave.

A week later, I received a thick manila envelope at my real estate office. The San Francisco postmark caught my eye.

I told our office manager that I wasn't feeling well and dashed out of the office. I parked my car a few blocks away and ripped open the envelope. Inside was a handwritten letter, a typed page that looked like some kind of business pitch, and a few copies of some magazine articles. I read the letter.

Dear Peggy,

I've tried not to think about you, but it hasn't worked. I can't help but think we'd be good together, but completely understand that you are happily married, so thought that I would, instead, make you a business proposition.

I would like to put together a proposal to produce the 50th anniversaries of the Bay Bridge and Golden Gate Bridge, which are coming up in the next two years. I know that you have some experience with fundraising, and I need a fundraiser. I've enclosed an outline of the proposal. I think our talents would complement each other. I've produced several events, and I know that you were successful in securing sponsors for your auction. If you think this sounds at all interesting, call me. If not, call me anyway and tell

*me I'm an asshole. Just kidding – go easy on me. This has been really
tough for me to get up the nerve to do.*

Yours,
George

*PS: The enclosed articles will give you some background on the
project.*

*PPS: A friend of mine is organizing volunteers for San Francisco's
Black and White Ball on June 12. Let me know if you want to
volunteer.*

I put the letter on my lap as every fiber in my body tingled.
*The Bay Bridge and Golden Gate Bridge anniversaries! Does he
really mean it?* The possibilities swam in my head. Was this just
a ploy to get me to spend time with him? Maybe. Would I ever
have another offer this great? Probably not.

That evening, I approached Paul as he read his new Porsche
manual.

"Some of my friends from our fund-raiser committee are
volunteering for the Black and White Ball on June 12," I lied.
"I thought I might volunteer, too." I tried not to sound very
enthusiastic.

"We're supposed to go to Tahoe that weekend," Paul said.
Normally, I looked forward to going up to the lake. Now the
thought of missing the Black and White Ball filled me with
dread.

"I could drive up the day after," I said.

He heaved a sigh. "I guess so." He shook his head
disappointedly. "Do you have to sign up for *everything*?"

* * *

June 12

It was late afternoon when I drove across the Bay Bridge, my directions to George's flat on the console, the black gown I wore to our San Ramon fund-raiser on the seat next to me. I glanced out at the Golden Gate Bridge in the distance and my heart skipped a beat. I was working at the Black and White Ball!

The two-story flat reminded me of Patrick's old place in The City.

I rang the buzzer and watched through the glass as George ran down to greet me.

"I can't believe you came!" George said as he walked behind me up the stairs.

"Would you like a glass of champagne?"

At the top of the stairs was a huge framed poster of the Beatles' album *A Hard Day's Night*. I smiled. "I love that!" I exclaimed. I toured the flat as he got my champagne. Nice detailed molding ... small black and white octagonal tiles in the bathroom ... a fireplace in one bedroom, and a view of downtown San Francisco from the other. My heart raced.

"Do you live here alone?" I called to him in the kitchen.

"No, I've got a roommate," George called back matter-of-factly. "He's got the room with the fireplace."

I walked to the window overlooking The City as he handed me my glass. The lights from the Transamerica Pyramid and other downtown buildings twinkled. Coit Tower beckoned from its hilltop. I sighed. It was the sight I'd always imagined myself having instead of a view of another suburban home.

"Are you hungry? I fixed us a little something to eat before we go." He led me to the kitchen, which had another great view of downtown. On the table were cloth napkins and a vase of lovely spring flowers. How could he *not* be gay?

He served tortellini with pesto and chicken. It was delicious.

Afterward, as we set our dishes on the kitchen counter, he leaned in to kiss me. I didn't protest. Gradually, we made our way to his bed. One thing led to another. We made love. When we finished, I began to cry.

He took me in his arms. "I'm so sorry. I shouldn't have asked you to come here: it was wrong. I knew I had this in mind."

I shook my head and sniffed. "No, it's not that," I took a breath. "I don't know how to explain this ... I'm happy, that's all."

We dressed and called for a cab. The Ball had bands in a number of different venues at the Civic Center. George was posted at City Hall and I was at the Green Room of Herbst Theater, in charge of giving directions to the bathroom and coat room. Mayor Feinstein and her husband stood talking with some people I recognized from the society pages. Boz Scaggs, looking dapper in tux and fedora, wandered in with his wife.

"How are you doing tonight?" he asked as they swept by.

"I couldn't be better," I replied, grinning.

When the clock struck twelve at the end of my shift, I ran like Cinderella to meet George at City Hall to watch the giant balloon drop. As the balloons were released, Boz Scaggs's band began to play, and we spun and dipped our way around the floor among the other revelers. For an hour, we were the Prince and Cinderella and then the music stopped. We were giddy as we entered the cab, but my carriage had turned back into a pumpkin.

"Can you stay tonight?" George asked.

"I better go home," I said reluctantly.

My mind was blank, my body numb as I drove back across the bridge. As I took the exit toward San Ramon on the freeway, I burst into tears. I was a piece of shit. I had just cheated on my husband and had enjoyed one of the best nights of my life! Paul might have his faults, but he was a good man, a good father. He, like my own father, would have done anything for me. I was a runny, stinky piece of shit.

I cried again the next morning as I drove through the foothills and into the forest beside the rocky river on Highway 50 on my way to meet Paul and Shane in Tahoe. I rolled down the windows and inhaled the fragrance of the pines. Paul was my soulmate, my best friend, my shelter from the storm. But in my heart, I had already decided. I was going to leave him.

Chapter 22

❦

Trouble on the Tarmac

Two weeks later we went camping with Paul's sister, Ann, and husband in the mountains. Shane was asleep in the camper with Ann. I leaned against Paul as we sat in a grounded rowboat in the dirt looking at the vast sky full of stars. I had never felt so empty. I started to cry.

"What's wrong now?" Paul asked. He was getting used to my emotional roller coaster.

My stomach tightened into a knot. Bile crept into my mouth. My head pounded as the words forced their way through my lips. "I want a separation," I said quietly.

Paul's body jerked behind me as though he had just been punched. "*What?*"

"I want a trial separation. I'm not happy anymore."

Paul stood up, bracing himself for a fight. "Just like that—a trial separation?" He threw up his hands in dismay.

As I stood to face him, the rowboat wobbled. "I've been telling you I'm unhappy for two years now."

He closed his eyes. When they opened, they were watery. I wanted to wrap my arms around him, to say I didn't mean it, that I'd stay and we'd be just fine, but I couldn't. Those words had disappeared. "I'll go to counseling," he offered. "We can work this out."

I leaned my head back and sighed. I had cried through the scenario of our breaking up so many times that I was cried out. I closed my eyes "I don't think it will help. I'm seeing someone else."

"Since *when?*" Paul asked angrily, his voice rising to a higher pitch.

It had only been a couple of weeks, but I wanted him to see the futility of trying. "For a few months."

He stepped out of the rowboat. His mouth twisted. "Who is it?"

I looked away.

"*Who?*"

"The lighting guy from the fund-raiser."

"*That* guy? You said he was gay!"

My answer took on a matter-of-fact tone. "I thought he was, but he's not."

"Stop seeing him!" he boomed.

In the past, I would have acquiesced. But now my dream of living in The City and creating something memorable was within reach. I wasn't about to turn back. "No!"

Paul's sister poked her head out from their trailer. "Everything okay out there?" In the silence of the mountain campsite, our voices were echoing.

We didn't speak again until the next day when we got home. I stood at the kitchen sink washing the camping dishes when Paul came in, his eyes red. "You *have* to try, Peg." He looked outside to Shane, who was swinging on the play set. "You owe it to us."

I rubbed my forehead for a full minute before answering. "Okay."

But no matter how hard I tried over the next few months, I couldn't change the way I felt. Though I tried to explain to Paul that I had to leave in order to rediscover the real me, as far as he was concerned, I was leaving him for another man.

At first, we fought over Shane—we each wanted custody. Finally, we agreed to split our weeks in half and alternate weekends. For the sake of continuity, we would keep Shane in the same preschool. I would drive back and forth from San Francisco on the days that I had him. Both of us agreed that, for Shane's sake, we wouldn't live with a romantic partner for at least a year.

Mom and Dad were terribly saddened by our breakup. They loved Paul—always had, and liked the couple they imagined we were. But they didn't try to talk me into staying. Mom, especially, understood my need to make a journey of my own.

I found a studio apartment in the Marina District with a bay window that framed the Golden Gate Bridge. That view became my inspiration, my reminder that I was at a gateway to my new life. Too bad the apartment was on the third floor with no elevator!

I loaded up the van with my clothes and other items: bedding, a lamp, my books, and art supplies. Paul helped me with the mattress; I didn't need box springs or a bed frame. Shane stood next to Paul at the curb, the house we had shared in the background. Dressed in matching T-shirt and shorts, his fine blond hair cut to just above his ears, he seemed to have grown inches overnight. I inhaled his fragrance of graham crackers, milk and Tide as I nuzzled his neck. *I'm not leaving you, little one: I'll always love you and will always take care of you.* Paul and I had done our best to explain what was happening, had even taken him to see my new apartment, but it was still confusing for a four-year-old mind.

"Mommy's gonna pick you up at preschool on Wednesday, Punkin, that's three days from today." I willed him not to cry. If he cried, I would, too.

"But Mommy, I don't want you to go to that place. Why can't you just stay here with Daddy and me?" Then Shane stooped to pick up a roly-poly bug inching its way across the sidewalk Maybe he'd forgotten his question. I kissed him on the head, and he looked up at me, "Mommy," he said, grabbing my arm with one hand while balancing the bug in a ball in the other, "stay here with us." The words, spoken so plainly, jabbed at my heart. I couldn't speak.

I gave Paul a pleading look. I was grateful when he said "Mommy loves you very much, honey. You'll get to see her soon."

I mouthed the words "thank you" to Paul. He smiled without smiling and shook his head. As I drove away, I studied the neighborhood where I'd lived for five years. The bushes had grown, and the trees were maturing. The lawns were neatly tended. It was a good neighborhood, a pretty neighborhood, a place where children could play and grow and be safe, but it wasn't me. It was a neighborhood where another kind of woman with other kinds of dreams settled in. But, women like me lived elsewhere, didn't they?

I had just turned onto the canyon road when I heard a "pop." The van started wobbling. I had a flat tire! I pulled to the side of the road. A couple of cows looked up as I closed the van's door. I looked at the tire. Definitely flat. I kicked it in frustration. Would I ever get out of San Ramon? I grabbed my purse and headed on foot toward the only house nearby, a football field away. The woman who answered the door eyed me warily.

"Can I use your phone?" I asked apologetically. "My car has a flat."

She ushered me into the kitchen and stood watching, arms folded, as I dialed.

Paul was surprised to hear my voice. "I'll be right there," he offered.

By the time I walked back to the van, Paul was already there. He glared at me, unsmiling. I had thought I couldn't feel any shittier about leaving. I was wrong.

"Hi, Mommy," Shane said nonchalantly from the backseat of the Porsche.

"Hi again, Sweetie," I said giggling nervously. "See, we told you I'd see you soon." Shane took one of the blanket fuzzies he always kept from his pocket. "Here Mommy," he said handing it to me, "You need this." I did indeed.

Mortified but appreciative, I watched as Paul changed the tire.

Though he resisted at first, he finally allowed me to hug him. "Thanks again," I said, gulping hard.

"Sure, anytime," he said, his eyes boring into mine.

Chapter 23

❧

My City Now

September, 1985

As I emerged from the Treasure Island tunnel halfway across the Bay Bridge, Sutro Tower, the Transamerica Pyramid building and Coit Tower lay before me bathed in sunlight. Streets teeming with cars and pedestrians, led down to the waterfront, where a stately red container ship headed out toward the Golden Gate with colorful windsurfers near the shore. I rolled down the windows and breathed in deep. The wind blew cool through my hair.

George and some friends helped me carry my things up the three flights of stairs as I apologized over and over for the lack of an elevator. That first week was a whirlwind of expeditions to Fort Mason for the Blues Festival, local restaurants, and hip dance clubs south of Market St. But I was anxious to lift off with my new career. As happy as I was to get out of real estate,

I now had a lot riding on winning the contracts for both bridge projects: Paul and I had never discussed splitting up our assets. Though I could cover my rent for a few months, after that, I had no idea what I was going to do.

Proposals for the Bay Bridge's fiftieth birthday celebration were due to the state office that controlled the bridge, the California Department of Transportation, "Caltrans," that November, so George and I had just over a month to come up with a detailed plan. Since the Golden Gate Bridge was completed six months after the Bay Bridge, The Golden Gate Bridge District would not be accepting proposals until the following spring.

George and I labored over the Bay Bridge proposal. Collaborating with a romantic partner was energizing, but difficult: as all of our conversations led back to how we could make the proposal better. Since George still worked at the lighting company full time, I spent my days gathering information at the Historical Society and public library (a process which today, with the Internet, seems incredibly archaic) and pulling innovative ideas from other event programs and brochures.

Since George had created many more events than I had, I hesitated to suggest changes to the proposal, but he insisted. "Your input is every bit as important as mine. I may have more experience at producing events, but you know more about how to raise money. If you're not willing to tell me when you think I'm wrong, I don't want to work with you."

* * *

January, 1986

George and I greeted all twenty-five members of the Bay Bridge Birthday Committee at the conference table, handing each of them one of our newly printed business cards. George set up the slide machine while I handed out copies of our proposal. As George spoke, my heart pounded.

After breezing through the first part of our proposal, George turned to me, my cue to start my part of the presentation.

I stood. The heat rose to my face. I began to sweat. "We'd like to propose a Bay Bridge poster contest for Bay Area schools ..." The birthday committee chair, Mike Foley, Jr., smiled and nodded. My heart calmed a little. *Slow it down: you're talking too fast!* "And a month-long display of the children's posters at the Oakland Museum." The aide to Oakland's mayor raised her eyebrows and nodded. "We're proposing billboards and PSAs featuring the bridge builders who are still alive." The whole group nodded. My voice became stronger. "And finally, we suggest a fireworks show to cap off the celebration." Half the group smiled. The other half looked skeptical.

"Fireworks shows are expensive," someone at the far end of the table said, "How do you propose we raise the money to pay for it?"

"Corporate sponsorship," I replied self-assuredly. *Right, like I've raised money for a fireworks show before.*

At the end of our presentation, the group gave us a big round of applause.

As George and I high-fived each other in the hallway, a rival group with slides and professional-looking storyboards passed us on their way to the conference room. My heart sank: What was I going to do if we didn't get this project?

One early morning in February we got the call: the committee wanted us to start immediately. There was only one hitch: they had no money to pay us. We would have to raise our fee through corporate sponsorships. I took a deep breath and turned to George. "I think I can do it."

* * *

April, 1986

I trolled Chestnut Street desperately hoping that someone would pull away from the curb. If only I could find a parking place on this block, I wouldn't have to carry Shane so far to my apartment. I'd opted not to get a garage space with my studio—I was barely eking by on my savings as it was.

No matter how much he seemed to enjoy the songs on the radio as we drove from San Ramon to The City, Shane always fell asleep in the car on the ride back. Somehow, it hadn't occurred to me that sharing custody of Shane would mean that at least three days a week I'd be making the trek across the Bay Bridge four times a day: to San Ramon to drop him off at preschool, back to The City for meetings, back again to San Ramon to pick him up, and back home to San Francisco. Depending on traffic, each round trip could take as long as two and a half hours, totaling five hours of driving in one day. I often wished I could just put the car on automatic pilot and curl up in the backseat with Shane.

I spotted a space. It was as close as I could possibly get to my apartment without being tagged for street cleaning or lack of a special neighborhood parking permit. I made a U-turn and pulled my car into position before seeing the person holding the parking place. I circled the block again, before resigning myself to parking three blocks away. I hoped Shane would wake up and walk part of the way. I unbuckled his seat belt and hoisted him onto my left arm. I slung the strap of my briefcase over my right shoulder. It was heavier since George and I had started working on our proposal to produce the Golden Gate Bridge celebration. Knowing that the bar would be higher for the internationally loved bridge, we'd spent even more hours on this proposal than the last and were including more bells and whistles. The deadline was approaching.

Damn! I'd forgotten I'd stopped for milk, bread, and cereal. I couldn't leave Shane alone in the apartment while I walked back to my car to get it. I scooped up the bag from the backseat with my right hand while balancing Shane on my left arm. City life could be a pain in the butt!

Luckily, Shane was light. But midway through the second flight of stairs, I had to stop and lean against the wall.

Shane lifted his head sleepily. "Are we almost there, Mommy?" he asked.

I nodded and said tiredly. "Yes, Punkin, we're almost there."

* * *

August, 1986

For the most part since I'd left the year before, Paul and I had been remarkably civil to each other. Paul started seeing a counselor and was dating a mutual friend, Debbie, who was planning to move in with him the following month. She, like George, was doing her best to warm up to Shane but was also getting rebuffed.

Once in a while, Paul and I would meet for dinner to discuss Shane, the bridge that spanned the distance between us. During one dinner, I let slip that I had started paying bills from my credit cards.

"Don't do that, Peg," he gently admonished. He had always been careful not to run up his credit card debt.

I shrugged. What could I do?

"You're not coming back, are you?" he asked, looking down.

"No," I said, looking away.

Paul sighed. "Then I think it's time we figure out what we're going to do."

Neither one of us was ready to get a divorce—a divorce seemed so final. Instead, we decided on a legal separation. We listed all of our assets and decided to split them down the middle: he would refinance the house and pay me half the equity, and I would take over the Porsche payments; he would continue to carry me on his company's health and car insurance, and I wouldn't ask for any money from his pension.

When Paul found an attorney, I thought it made sense for me to use the same one. After all, we'd already worked everything out. We'd probably save some money. When we went in for our appointment, Paul and I sat across from each other at the table. "Ms. Kennedy, it's unusual for me to represent both spouses in a separation," the attorney said as he sat down, "I must tell you that it may not be in your best interest."

"I know. Other people have told me the same thing. But I trust Paul, and I think he trusts me," I said looking at Paul. He smiled tightly.

After we'd gone over everything, the attorney cleared his throat. "I have to say something to the two of you which I don't believe I've ever said to anyone else in this situation: I think there's a good chance that you're going to get back together some day. You're just so decent to each other."

Paul and I laughed. "That's because we've known each other since we were kids," Paul said. We exchanged glances. For a moment we were together again on my parent's front porch.

Bridges had begun dominating my life. The Birthday Committee had set up an office for us in the basement of the TransBay bus terminal with desks, a copier, a couple of typewriters, and a secretary. The copier worked about half the time and so did the secretary. The corridor outside the office smelled of urine. Homeless people often wandered in to chat.

Finding sponsors was much more difficult than I had imagined. George and I brought in another fund-raiser and event producer to help us. Though we'd secured a cash sponsor for the children's poster contest and a few "in-kind" sponsors for printing and wine, we were still beating the bushes. We only earned a commission on cash sponsorships. Time was running out!

A few months earlier, our proposal for the Golden Gate Bridge celebration had been rejected in favor of a razzle-dazzle proposal from a major New York event producer. With a hair-raising sponsorship goal of $20 million, they had proposed not only fireworks but also a concert with Tony Bennett and permanent lighting for the bridge!

In contrast, the Bay Bridge Committee was scaling back their plans due to lack of funds, keeping only the low-cost events such as the antique car parade across the bridge, the dinner for the bridge builders, and the giant birthday cake painted on the huge anchorage in the middle of the suspension side of the bridge.

Unless they had seen one of the donated outdoor billboard ads or heard the promotions on a local radio station for a free toll on the actual bridge birthday, the people of the Bay Area were unaware that the Bay Bridge Fiftieth Birthday celebration was even approaching, that is until the day when the *San Francisco Chronicle* ran a full-page cover story comparing the two bridge celebrations. On the left was an old black-and-white photo of the Bay Bridge, making it look like the ugly stepsister bridge. The Bay Bridge Birthday events that were listed looked just as dowdy and boring. George and I were plugged in as the event's producer and fund-raiser just above where it mentioned that only $20,000 had been raised. Nothing was listed under our successes. On the right was a rendering taken from the New York producer's proposal showing the dramatically lit Golden Gate Bridge bathed in a colorful explosion of fireworks. Under "Producer" was a half-page-long list of their successful productions, which included Super Bowl parties, that summer's blowout Statue of Liberty celebration, and much, much more.

I was mortified, but couldn't turn back: regardless of how colorless the Bay Bridge celebration might be, we had committed to do it. And, at that point, I had no other way to produce income.

* * *

One month later

George's roommate moved out, and I happily moved in. It was nice not to have to drive from my place to his. Time was tight as the Bay Bridge Birthday approached—we barely had time to breathe between meetings, phone calls, and production of print materials, invitations, and public service announcements.

Our romantic relationship, like our business relationship, was egalitarian. Unlike Paul, George was willing to share cooking, cleaning, and laundry chores. Now that I was far from my former role of a traditional mother, I no longer felt the need to do it all. I welcomed his help.

George and I shared the bedroom with the fireplace while Shane slept in George's old bedroom. Though weekday mornings were rushed as I scurried to get Shane up and into the car so he wouldn't be late for kindergarten in San Ramon, on Saturday mornings, the three of us always made time to curl up on the couch to watch *Pee Wee's Playhouse*.

I loved the fact that George was still a kid at heart. And I loved the fact that he openly cried when something moved him. What I didn't love was his drinking. When we'd lived apart, in the evenings, we'd always have one or two glasses of wine. Now that we were living together, I saw that after those two glasses, he usually drank hard liquor. I worried he was becoming an alcoholic, but was too overwhelmed by our workload to address it.

Though George enjoyed my family, my family's baggage— Mom's mental illness, Joan's murder, and Dad's growing disorientation—seemed to make him uneasy. When he made disparaging comments about his aunt, who was also mentally ill, I took them as an affront to my mother. In my mind, George was judging my mom for being sick: something that Paul had never done. To me, it was an unforgivable offense.

Sue called me one day shortly after I moved in. Glenn, who'd been on vacation in Hawaii, had called her that morning to ask her to pick him up at the airport. But when Sue arrived at the gate, Glenn was in a wheelchair, wearing an oxygen mask on his face and a lei around his neck, being pushed by an attendant down the ramp. When Sue asked Glenn if he'd come down with a bad case of asthma, he replied that the doctor in Hawaii thought it was meningitis.

Sue sighed deeply on the other end of the phone.

"Would they have let him on the plane with meningitis?" I asked skeptically.

Sue was silent. Finally, she spoke again. "I asked if he wanted me to take him to the doctor, but he said no, he just wanted to go home. I dropped him off at his apartment and offered to stay, but he said he'd be fine. I just talked with him a few minutes ago. He *does* sound better," she said, her voice dropping.

"So do you really think he has meningitis?" The familiar feeling of dread in regard to Glenn's sex life rose in the pit of my stomach. I closed my eyes as I waited.

"Peg ... I think Glenn has AIDS." Though I expected it, the news was unbearable. I put the receiver down on the table, covered my face with my hands, and cried. In 1986, getting AIDS was a death sentence.

"Peg?" Sue's voice called from a distance.

I picked up the phone. "Should we just ask him?" I sputtered.

"He'll tell us when he wants us to know."

* * *

By our Bay Bridge Birthday committee meeting in mid-October—only one month to go before the event—I had still not secured any additional corporate sponsorships. Since our fee was 15 percent of sponsorships, and I had brought in only $20,000, George and I had each earned a grand total of $1,500. Mike Foley, the committee chair, said, "Your Company has worked hard to make our celebration a success. The billboards and bus banners are up, the children's posters are on display at the Oakland Museum, and our print materials are all ready to go. I only wish we had a budget so that we could pay you what you deserve." His words, though kind, only made me feel worse. It had been my job to raise the money for the celebration.

George got his digs in that night. "Gosh, I don't know ... I'm having trouble figuring out how to spend all of the money that I've earned working on this event for oh ... let's see ... eight months now? What's my portion again ... $1,500! Let's see," he said pulling out his calculator, "Oh boy, that's $187.50 a month!" George had another job, and I didn't. Normally his sarcasm made me laugh until it hurt. Now it just hurt.

A few days later it was hot and humid. Our office felt like a sauna and smelled like a latrine. The smell suited my mood: with less than a month to go and no prospects for additional sponsorship dollars, my career was in the toilet. George, having finished his lighting company appointments, had come in to, as he called it, "dial for dollars." He took off his suit jacket and loosened his tie. When the phone rang, he picked up. As he listened, he sat up straighter. He furiously wrote something down. His face was animated as he hung up the phone. "That was Jim Souza," he said. "His family is originally from Oakland. They're upset that everyone's making fun of the Bay Bridge celebration. They own a fireworks company and want to donate a $250,000 fireworks show to our event!"

I pumped my fist in the air. We might not make any money, but the event would be a success!

Once word got out that the fireworks show was donated, others wanted to donate too. Within days, a sound company donated massive speakers to set up along the Embarcadero so that crowds could hear the music for the fireworks sky show; a company kicked in giant searchlights to station on the bridge, and the navy and coast guard agreed to provide barges and safety boats. A popular local radio station called to say they would do hundreds of free promotional spots for the event.

On November 2, the opening of a Bay Bridge Exhibit was followed by a dinner at the Officer's Club on Treasure Island for the men who built the bridge. On November 12, the Bay Bridge was closed to all traffic as a parade of cars circa 1936 motored across, reenacting the day the bridge opened fifty years earlier.

The weather was balmy the following Saturday morning as crowds began to gather along the waterfront near the bridge. By late afternoon, tens of thousands of people jammed BART stations to make their way to the Embarcadero for the huge fireworks display, dubbed the largest display ever on the West Coast. Some BART stations had to be shut down for fear that their platforms would collapse from the mass of body weight. George and I were ecstatic. "Thank God for the Souzas!" we cheered gleefully.

The Souza family invited George and me and our families to enjoy the show from a cruise boat they'd rented. Patrick, busy with a project in New York, couldn't make it. Mom, her sense of adventure vanished due to psychotic drugs and unrealized dreams, stayed home with a runny nose. Glenn, who was feeling better, brought Dad. Despite his growing forgetfulness, my father picked up on the excitement of the crowd and grew animated as we waited to embark. The sun was setting as George, Shane, Glenn, Dad, and I moved with George's family and a throng of other guests up the ramp and onto the boat. Sue, arriving late from work, ran up the ramp and jumped aboard just before the cruise boat left the dock.

Hundreds of thousands of people lined the Embarcadero shore as the sky grew dark. Traffic on the bridge and along the Embarcadero freeway came to a stop as people got out of their cars to watch. Boats of all shapes and sizes filled the Bay. As the music began, Roman candle fireworks lit the giant birthday candles on the six-story tall birthday cake painted on the anchorage of the bridge ... the searchlights went on ... music started playing ... and the fireworks show began. As we stood on the deck of the boat, each burst above us seemed larger and more colorful than the last. The pyramid building and Coit tower glowed, and the checkerboard buildings of downtown San Francisco seemed to pulse to the beat of the music. Sue was cheering. Shane was mesmerized. Glenn was laughing. Dad was grinning.

I had created something memorable. After the finale, with chrysanthemums, palms and starbursts exploding one right after the other, a necklace of lights appeared all along the suspension cables, and our bridge to The City became a twinkling runway. The crowd went wild.

Chapter 24

❦

Falling Apart

March, 1987

Soon after the necklace of lights illuminated the Bay Bridge on its fiftieth birthday, a group of media people from Bay Area newspapers, radio stations, and television started a campaign called "Keep the Change," which encouraged people to pay an extra quarter over their seventy-five-cent bridge toll toward helping Caltrans make the necklace of lights permanent. A month or so later, Bob Halligan, the Public Affairs Director for Caltrans who oversaw the Bay Bridge Birthday celebration, called me in for a meeting. A few other Bay Bridge Committee members sat around a small table.

Bob wasted no time. He pointed to a large stack of canvas bags in the corner of his office. "You see those bags over there?"

I nodded.

"Well, ever since they started that Keep the Change campaign, our toll takers have accepted the quarters, but they haven't known what to do with them. Finally, one of the supervisors had the bright idea to bring all the bags here to my office," he chortled. "We think that so far we've collected over eighty thousand dollars! Obviously, the public wants these permanent lights. We're guessing we're going to need about eight hundred thousand. The California legislature will pass a bill to fund part of it, but we still need someone to raise the balance of the money we need from corporate sponsors. Would you be interested? We'd be willing to pay you a retainer."

I assumed they wanted George more than me. "I'll have to check with George to make sure he's available."

"Uh ... well the truth is ... we'd like to just work with you. George rubbed a few people the wrong way," he said. George's sarcasm had a way of doing that.

I didn't hesitate. "I'd love to!"

My career had officially taken off.

Though I could tell he was disappointed, George congratulated me on getting the project. "I know you'll do a great job, girlfriend," he said hugging me. I still wasn't sure if I liked that name—girlfriend—it was edgy and fun, but unlike babe or honey or sweetheart, it was distancing.

* * *

July, 1987

The media's Keep the Change campaign got the word out about the Bay Bridge permanent lighting. By July, between in-kind and cash donations, I was halfway to my goal. I was overjoyed. George, now busy marketing a documentary about the Golden Gate Bridge, took me out to dinner to celebrate.

My career was coming together, but my family was falling apart.

The phone rang one morning at 7:00 a.m. "Peg, I'm so glad you're there," Mom said anxiously. This was weird. I usually got anxious calls from Dad about Mom.

"Honey," she continued, speaking lower than normal, "Daddy left in the car over an hour ago to get some milk. He should have been back by now."

"Maybe he ran into someone he knows at the store," I suggested.

"Could be," Mom's voice drifted even lower, "but ever since he lost the car a couple of months ago I worry. You know we finally had to call the Castro Valley police to help us find it …"

"I know. You told me it was parked in someone's stall at the apartment across the street …"

"Can you imagine? Our apartment buildings don't even look alike. I wish I could see so I could drive. But the doctor says that … "

"I know, Mom. He says that as long as you're on the medication, your vision will be impaired." We'd been through this once before. It was early: without coffee, I was a little testy. We agreed she'd call me back in ten minutes if Dad wasn't back.

I hung up the phone and rubbed my eyes, a habit I'd developed over the years thinking it would help me to see. It still didn't work. I was practically blind until I put my contacts in. I shuffled over to the kitchen counter and flipped on the coffeepot, having gotten it ready the night before. I was my mother's daughter.

A few minutes later, the phone rang again.

"Peg," Mom said frantically, "The Danville police have Daddy." She sniffed. "They got a call that someone was in a cul-de-sac driving round and round in circles. They said Daddy couldn't even remember his name …" she blew her nose. "They had to ask him for his wallet to get it."

I volunteered to go get him. Glenn went with me.

Glenn and I pulled in to the court at around the same time. Daddy sat looking absently out the window from the backseat of the police car. A few neighbors with coffee mugs chatted on one of the lawns while some children played tag. Three policemen stood talking next to the car in which Dad sat. They watched us park. Glenn's shirt looked two sizes too big. He took my hand, and we walked together toward the car. Through the window, Daddy waved and smiled as though greeting us at his front door.

One of the policemen opened the back door. Daddy's legs were wobbly. He had wet his pants. I grabbed one of his elbows, and Glenn grabbed the other. Dad raised his eyebrows and gave a mock surprised grin like he always did when he was trying to make the best of a situation. "Well, fancy meeting you here!" he exclaimed. Glenn and I cracked up. We had to catch the laughs when we could.

One of the policemen stepped forward. He seemed appalled that we were laughing. "You need to take better care of your father, you two," he said. "He shouldn't be driving."

Glenn and I nodded solemnly. Glenn signed the release paper and handed it back to the policeman. We adjusted our grip on Dad's elbows and guided him to the front seat of my car.

*   *   *

September, 1987

Two months later, it was Glenn we were worried about. He called Sue in the middle of the night struggling for breath. Sue rushed over to his apartment in Oakland—no small feat from Santa Rosa. Glenn's skin, Sue said, felt hot enough to singe her finger. She took him to the hospital. There, he finally admitted he had AIDS. Sue called Pat, who flew out from New York. The day Glenn came home from the hospital, I took Shane to see him. Glenn lived on the second floor of a square stucco 1960s apartment building. His furniture was futuristic Jetson style: orange chairs with sleek lines ready for take off; a boxy lime green couch with spindly legs; and a silver starburst clock on the wall. His expansive veranda, dotted with cactus plants and chaise lounges, had a view of Lake Merritt. He liked living alone. At that time, Kaiser had supplied him with a hospital bed which was squeezed into his bedroom beside his blonde wood rectangular chest of drawers and black metal chair.

Patrick opened the door when I knocked. We hugged, and he took Shane by the hand. "It's high time I showed you how to play my favorite game," Pat's lower incisor wrapped round his upper canine as he smiled. I followed them into where Glenn lay propped against some pillows on his bed. Glenn's eyes twinkled as Shane jumped up to give him a hug. My eyes met Glenn's. He smiled comfortingly as he put out his hand. How much longer would he be alive? *Don't cry.*

"Hi, honey." I forced a smile as I took his hand and sat down beside him.

Pat pulled out a piece of paper from Glenn's drawer and folded it. He grabbed two pens and gave one to Shane who sat next to him at the end of the bed. "Okay, here's the game: I draw a scribble like this," Pat said, his pen flying around the paper, "and you make a picture out of it," he said, pulling Shane in.

The six-year-old Shane twisted his mouth. "I'm not a very good *draw*-er."

"Sure you are! You just don't know it yet." Pat handed Shane the scribble, and Shane went to work with his pen.

A balloon bouquet hovered over Glenn's desk. "Where'd ya get *that?*" I asked Glenn as playfully as I could.

"Oh, my students sent it yesterday when they heard I wouldn't be at school for a while ..." his voice trailed downward as he looked out the window.

I squeezed his hand. "It's lovely—suitable for Winnie the Pooh," I said. He squeezed my hand back and smiled a wrinkled smile.

Shane wasn't used to drawing without an eraser. Unhappy with his picture, he attempted to cross it out. "No, no, no," Pat admonished lightheartedly. "Let's see it!"

Shane showed him reluctantly. "Perfect!" Pat exclaimed. "I see a big monster and a little fish."

Shane was elated. It was just what he'd drawn. "You do?"

Patrick nodded, grinning. "For that great picture, you get to take a ride on my knees. Bet you can't stay on!"

Shane, small and light for his age, eagerly hopped on Pat's lap just above his knees.

"Okay, now hold on," Pat cautioned. Shane grabbed the metal arms of the chair. As Patrick's right leg bounced up, Shane giggled. When Pat's left leg went up, Shane's fine hair floated in the air. Pat's legs jigged faster. Left leg, right, right right then up left, then *waayyy* up right until Shane let go of the arms of the chair and slipped off Patrick's bony knees.

Patrick had won the game. "*Ha ha ha haaaaa*," he yelled, á la Captain Hook.

Glenn coughed, his whole body wracking in spasms to expel the foreign interloper in his lung. When he was done coughing, he fell back limply onto his pillow, sweat dripping from his brow.

I took a tissue from the box and held it to Glenn's mouth. He dutifully spit the small green phlegm into the tissue. I threw the tissue into a gallon-sized baggie with several others and dabbed his brow with a wet washcloth as I'd seen Sue do. He smiled briefly in thanks before closing his eyes.

"Poor Grinchie," Patrick said.

"Poor Grinchie," repeated Shane in solemn agreement.

There was a tap on the front door. I went to answer. Sue, wearing a trench coat, entered carrying a small brown bag. Pat and Shane came to see who it was. Shane ran to hug his aunt.

"Hello, my little Shane," she said smiling. "How did you get so tall?"

Shane stood up straighter and smiled.

Sue opened the brown bag. "I got this from a friend of mine;" she said in her medical expert voice, "It's one of the new trial drugs that I told Glenn about. He said he wanted to try it."

Glenn rolled over. Catching his breath, he managed to get out, "Oh, thank God you got it, Sue."

"Well, another country heard from," Sue said, surprised like all of us that Glenn was awake. We all laughed at Sue's use of Mom's phrase. Had Mom and Dad known that Glenn was so sick they would have been at Glenn's apartment, too. Glenn had made us promise not to tell them. I didn't know whether he was protecting them or avoiding finally telling my parents he was gay.

Sue walked into Glenn's bedroom. "Donna said that her friend Doug, who has pneumasistis, too, was able to breathe normally again after just a few days," Sue said with a wide smile that I could tell she didn't feel as she sat down on the bed. "She said to take one in the morning along with some food if you can get it down."

"Oh, what a relief," Glenn said, gurgling.

"So, Griiinnnnch," Pat said playfully, "Why don't you just take a little nap and we'll sit right outside your room until you've had some rest."

"I'll be happy to do that if you would just adjust my pillows," Glenn said with a toothy smile. Breathing laboriously, he bent forward. Patrick laid the two flat long pillows on the bottom and the softer pillows on top. "Princess Poopoo's pillows are ready for her." Pat batted his lashes.

Glenn laughed briefly as he lay back.

"Princess Poopoo needs her rest now," Pat said as he led Shane out of the room and closed the door softly behind them. Only then did he allow a look of deep sadness to take over his expression.

Chapter 25

✥

Lighting Our Bridge to The City

By that October, I had helped to secure, in cash and in-kind donations, the amount that Caltrans needed to begin installing the permanent lighting on both the cantilever and suspension sides of the Bay Bridge, and I was now helping to produce Art Agnos's mayoral inaugural celebration in the Civic Auditorium. The theme was "Neighborhoods of San Francisco." Everything had to be donated. Over the next few weeks, my ears became sore to the touch from so much pleading over the phone.

By Christmas, Glenn was smoking pot to increase his appetite, and was taking AZT, which boosted his energy level and gave his face a pinkish glow. "I get to hand out the presents," he said smiling as he sat on the burnt-orange chair next to Mom and Dad's fake Christmas tree. Red and blue bulbs hung from its plastic boughs along with the folded beret with button eyes and red sock with candy-cane nose that Joan had made almost twenty years before.

Patrick was finishing up creating a designer showroom in New York and couldn't be there, but the rest of us were. "This one says it's for Daddy," Glenn crossed the room to hand the present to him. Dad, in a fog most of the time now, put the present on his lap.

"Open it, Daddy." Mom patted his knee. "That one's from the Baby."

The word seemed to kindle a memory. Daddy smiled and opened the gift: a bottle of cologne. He set it on the table without acknowledging Mom. Mom crossed her hands in her lap. Sometimes now, it seemed, the pitiful return on her attempts to bring him back were too painful.

"And this one's for Sister Sue from the Grinch." Glenn handed it to her. It looked like a book.

Sue untied the ribbon and tore open the tissue. "*Candide*! Where did you find it?" she asked excitedly.

"I have ways," he said in his best Grinch voice. His voice changed back to Glenn's. "Actually, it's mine. I wanted to give it to you." There was a pregnant pause as the finality of that statement hit all three of us. Sue turned away.

"Pegs ..." Glenn said, handing me a rectangular package.

Inside were the three James Clavell novels that Glenn had been telling me I should read.

"Those are some big books!" Dad exclaimed.

I'd seen the books on Glenn's bookshelf. I hugged him. "I'll read them and give them back to you."

"No need to," he replied.

* * *

A few days later, I rushed to answer the phone. With only ten days left before Agnos' inauguration, I was anxious to tie up all the loose ends. I hoped it was one of the big name comedians I'd asked to MC one of the stages. But it was Mom.

"Honey, I'm exhausted. Your father wanders around all night, and I'm so afraid he's going to go out once I fall asleep. There's an Alzheimer's day care center here in Castro Valley, and they said we could start bringing Daddy over there a couple of days a week. Do you think you could take him there for me, Peg?"

"Sure, Mom," I said, anxiously. I was having a hard time balancing my full tray as it was. "When do you want me to take him?"

"Tomorrow?"

"Uhhh, sure, Mom. What time?" I had a meeting scheduled at 11:00 a.m. with about fifty of the performers for the inaugural.

"They open at ten o'clock. If he could stay there from ten to three I'd have a chance to get some sleep," Mom said hopefully.

If I picked Dad up at 9:30, he'd be a little early, but maybe they'd take him. Then I could come back across the bridge, park, and be in my meeting a little bit before 11:00. "Okay, Mom, I can do it."

"Oh, honey," Mom said with relief, "that would be wonderful."

I got stuck on the phone in the morning and picked Dad up by 10:15. When I got him to the day care center I had to fill out some paperwork. I thought about calling George, but didn't know where to reach him. Very few people carried cell phones in those days. Traffic was bad on the bridge. By the time I walked into the meeting at 11:30, some of the entertainers had already left. The room was chaotic. George, working on the lighting and sound in a different room, caught me in the hallway.

"I can't *believe* you're late!" he seethed. I was making him look bad. too.

"I'll tell you about it later," I said through a forced smile.

"I'm so sorry I'm late," I said to the group.

A woman wearing a beaded vest and head scarf representing a Russian dance group stood up and wagged her finger at me. "You expect us to work pro bono, and yet you don't respect us by being on time!" she said in a thick accent. The room was silent.

I dug deep in my memory, *"Eezveeneetya, Poyzhalusta"* I said in Russian, hand to my heart. *Please forgive me.*

Her mouth fell open. The room was abuzz as the woman conferred with the person next to her. She turned to me and smiled. "Horosho."

I said a silent thank-you to "Gospodeen" Stern. All those years of Russian had finally come in handy. The room was mine.

* * *

January, 1988

Art Agnos's Inaugural Party was a success. But things were looking grim for my family.

Dad, at sixty-one, had found a permanent hiding place in his mind. His body began to shut down as well. Though we hired someone to come to the apartment to help, she often wasn't there when Dad fell or needed to get out of bed. In shame and despair, Mom put Dad in a convalescent hospital. She cried as I drove her home. "Please don't put me in one of those places, honey. I'd rather just die."

Two weeks later, Dad was transferred to the hospital with pneumonia. The following day, I pushed the lever on Dad's hospital bed so that he could sit up. When he finished coughing, Mom held a tissue to his mouth so he could spit. Dad caught his breath and leaned back against the pillow. I scooted a chair over next to the bed for Mom to sit in.

"They gave me my own channel changer." Dad held it up for us to see. He glanced at the man who was sharing his room and motioned for us to lean closer. "He didn't get one," he whispered, smiling as though he'd just won a prize.

A series of television stations whizzed by as Dad pushed down on the channel changer. He stopped when he heard a familiar song playing in a commercial for an oldies album. "I like this," he said, as though hearing the song for the first time.

"That's Glenn Miller, Daddy," Mom said taking his hand. "We used to dance to this."

Daddy started to hum along, "*da da da da da da da da* ..." The cloud cover in his eyes seemed to clear. Mom joined in.

Dad's roommate turned over in his bed, "That's a good old song," he said, his voice raspy, "Moonlight Serenade."

Mom looked at the man and smiled. "I always had to make this one dance," she said, nodding at Dad with her head, "I had to drag him onto the dance floor."

Daddy grinned and shook his head, "I never liked to dance. Everybody looks at you!" It was the most lucid thing he'd said in a month.

One day the following week, Mom was sick with a cold so I went to see Dad by myself. I heard talking coming from the room as I approached. I peeked in ... the bed next to Dad was empty. Dad's face was animated. "Hey, Peg, so glad you stopped by! I want you to meet Jake, an old buddy of mine from the army."

I'd finally get to meet one of the guys that Dad had fought with in the war! Jake ... Jake ... Jake was the one that joined the army at the same time as Daddy ... they'd gone to the recruiting station together when they were just seventeen. They'd jumped out of planes together ... Jake ... wait a minute ... wasn't Jake the one who'd gotten shot down? There was no one around. I knocked on the bathroom door, but it was empty. "Did he step out for a second, Daddy?" I asked.

"No, Peg," he laughed. "He's right here!" Dad pointed to the side of the bed.

Tears formed in my eyes. "Hi, Jake," I nodded and smiled in that direction.

Dad grinned. "Jake says that there's a bunch of guys that hang out together every night down at Mulligan's on Forty-first Avenue, right down by where Jake and I used to live. Jake says he'll come and pick me up tomorrow, and we'll go there together."

Daddy died peacefully in his sleep two days later. The next morning, I went with Mom to the mortuary to plan the rosary and pick out the casket. After that, we went to pick out his headstone.

A few days later, I held Mom's hand in the front row of the chapel at Dad's rosary. Patrick sat on her other side. Sue and Glenn, arriving late, scooted in next to Pat. Later I learned that Sue had had a drink with Glenn to buck him up. I thought our row smelled an awful lot like brandy.

The Rosary was well attended by family and friends. Paul brought Shane. Since George sat with me, they sat in a separate row. Midway through the service, Shane squeezed in between Mom and me. I held his hand. I didn't cry. Afterward, Paul hugged Mom, Glenn, Sue, and Pat. When he hugged me, I burst into tears. I knew he felt Dad's loss almost as much as we did. I felt safe crying in his arms.

After the ceremony at the gravesite, Mom was given a flag by a man dressed in military uniform. On Dad's granite headstone was etched:

JOHN THOMAS KENNEDY

MAY 9, 1926–JANUARY 27, 1988

STAFF SERGEANT, U.S. ARMY

* * *

February, 1988

"Peg, you'll never guess who just called me," Mom said over the phone a few weeks after Dad died.

From her lack of enthusiasm, I could tell that I really didn't want to know, but I played along. "Who?"

"Your cousin Michael." Ah yes, my cousin Michael, who, along with my Aunt Noreen, had helped himself to Mom's and Aunt Marie's inheritance.

"He asked you for money, didn't he?"

"Nope." I heard Mom taking a deep puff from her cigarette and exhaling it. This was serious. "He asked if he, Joanne, and their kids, could move in with me."

"Holy shit!" It was worse than I thought. "Mom, you're not going to do it, are you?"

Another deep puff … another full exhale. "Peg, he's got four little kids. Both Michael and Joanne are in between jobs. They've been living at St. Elizabeth's Church ever since they lost their apartment a couple of weeks ago, but the church has a two-week limit. He says they have nowhere to go."

"Mom, this is the guy that stole your inheritance."

"Honey, I know. He says he hasn't been able to live with himself ever since," Mom replied.

"Well then, how is it that he never called you to tell you he was sorry? He never even made it to Daddy's funeral."

There was silence on the other end of the phone. I could see her swirling her cigarette around in the ashes.

"He says the children are really well behaved." She had made up her mind.

"Have you told anyone else?" I asked. Surely one of my siblings could talk her out of this.

"Not yet." Naturally she'd called me, the soft touch, before anyone else.

"Mom, call Sue before you tell him yes." Sue could make the case against taking them in better than I could.

As I hung up, I pictured Michael and his family with their suitcases and cardboard boxes on Mom's doorstep. Of course she'd take them in. I would, too. For that matter, so would Sue.

* * *

Joanne and Mike slept with their two youngest children, aged two and five, in Mom's guest room, while their two older children, aged seven and nine, took turns sleeping on the living room couch and floor.

For once, Michael had told the truth: his kids were the quietest, most well-behaved children I'd ever met. At night, the younger kids sat on their parents' laps on the couch while the older kids sat at their feet watching television. Michael peeled oranges and divided them into six portions for a snack. Mom, never a big fan of TV, retired to her bedroom at night to listen to the radio.

Shortly after they moved in, I stopped by, said my hellos and followed Mom into her bedroom. "So what's it like having a family in your house again?" I asked.

Mom shrugged. "They're pretty quiet. Mike and Joanne are gone all day—I suppose looking for jobs. They take the younger kids with them, and the older kids are in school. They buy their own food and fix their own meals. They're not much trouble, really. But I did kind of like having the place to myself," she said, her mouth a straight line.

"Any word on jobs yet?" I asked hopefully.

"I'm sure they'll find something pretty soon."

* * *

By March, the lights on the Bay Bridge were almost completely installed. True to his word, Bob Halligan called me. A dinner/press event at the World Trade Club was planned for the first week in May.

By the end of April, Glenn was in the hospital again. Though Head Royce had agreed to a leave of absence due to "meningitis," it was pretty obvious that Glenn would not be able to go back to teaching. His fever had come back, and breathing was more of a struggle than ever. Keeping on weight had become almost impossible—even brushing his teeth made him gag. Most cruel of all, his eyes burned when he read. But as far as Mom knew, Glenn was off on a two-week camping trip with the school.

The party at the World Trade Club came together nicely, with California Governor Deukmejian, San Francisco Mayor Agnos, and Oakland Mayor Wilson in attendance to flip the giant switch that would illuminate the permanent lights on the bridge. Two local radio talk show hosts were there to MC. A special award was given to the Souza family for the fireworks show they'd donated eighteen months before.

The temporary lighting that had illuminated the bridge during its birthday party had been off for almost a year. The public was clamoring: they wanted their Cinderella bridge back! The new lights were secretly tested during the day to keep the public in suspense.

By some strange twist of fate, the Saturday morning of the dinner, Glenn was moved to a room overlooking the Bay Bridge. As he told me later, the nurse came around early that evening to give him yet another shot of God knew what in his butt. She mentioned that the sunset was lovely and wouldn't he like for her to open the shades? He'd like that, yes, thank you, he replied. When she opened them, he saw that she was right—the sunset was beautiful. As the sun went down and the sky darkened, his gaze drifted to the bridge, where the magical necklace of lights created a twinkling runway into The City. *Ah yes, he thought before floating off to sleep, Pegs lit our bridge forever ... she lit it just for me.*

Chapter 26

❦

Who's Zoomin' Who?

May, 1988

The sicker Glenn became, the more frustrated I became with the lack of a concerted effort to find a cure for his disease. I began working on a proposal for an AIDS-benefit concert. As with the bridge project, my ignorance only made me bolder.

Around that same time San Francisco's Chinese Chamber of Commerce asked George and me to give them a proposal to produce their annual San Francisco Chinese New Year Parade. I was beside myself. Here was an event recognized around the world in which I might finally be able to use my major in Asian Studies! I eagerly began gathering information to put our proposal together. But just a week later, George got another call.

"Hey, girlfriend," George said one night when he got home from work. By the drop in his voice, I could tell something was up. He poured us each a glass of wine and brought them in to the couch where I was reading the newspaper.

He took my hand. Now I was really nervous. "Peg, you know how I've always talked about wanting to work with the guy that did the 1984 opening and closing ceremonies for the LA Olympics?"

I nodded.

"I found out that his company is looking for a marketing director." George had been tired of his job for a long time, but we still weren't making enough money to live on—I was living in part on the equity I got from the house.

"I applied for the job," he went on trying to hide his excitement. "They want me to come in for an interview."

"That's great! I know you'll get it!" This was good news. Why all the drama?

"There's only one problem ..." he said.

"What?" I asked, dreading whatever was coming.

"It's in Southern California, in Palos Verdes." His face scrunched as he awaited my reaction.

"Achhhh! I can't move to Southern California! I've got Shane and Glenn's sick. I can't leave!" I shook my head. My dream was in San Francisco, not LA.

"Okay," he sighed. "So we'll have to have a long-distance romance."

I grimaced.

"Peg," he said, taking my hand, "I'm thirty-five. If I don't go after my dream now, I'm never going to achieve it."

I certainly understood that.

I scooted away. "What about the Chinese New Year Parade?" I asked. It would be a steady contract for at least a couple of years.

"You can handle it, Peg. You've proven that with the Light Up the Bridge contract."

What could I say? "Good luck." I said, my stomach in a knot.

* * *

By the end of May, Michael and Joanne had still not found jobs. Mom called me one afternoon when they were gone. "Honey, do you think I've been duped again?"

I exhaled loudly. "Mom, I'm going to come over and talk with Michael. I'll tell him it's time to go."

"Honey, the kids." The discussion was over.

She called me again the following week.

"The saga continues, Peg." Mom said taking a puff from her cigarette.

"What now?" I asked wearily.

"Michael and Joanne told me a couple of nights ago that they've both landed jobs at a photo studio, and they've found a house to rent in Dublin." She said evenly.

"That's great!" I cheered. "When do they move out?"

Mom inhaled again. This couldn't be good. "They asked to borrow five thousand dollars."

"*What?*" I raged.

"I told them I didn't have that kind of money," Mom said defensively, "but they said, 'Sure you do. You've got credit cards, haven't you?'"

Mom was proud that she had recently paid off her credit cards. "Honey, I didn't think it was possible, but they said I could write a check on my credit card account and they would make the monthly payments."

"Mom, listen to me," I said, as though holding her face still so she'd pay attention, "Michael will never pay you back. Your payments will be exorbitant. You're barely getting by on Daddy's pension and social security as it is!"

"Oh, honey," Mom said resignedly, "Susie said the same thing."

"You talked to Sue?" I asked hopefully.

"Yes," she said with a sigh, "and she was not exactly enthusiastic either."

I opened my mouth, but Mom broke in. "Honey, Michael and Joanne drove me to the bank yesterday. I gave them the check. They moved out last night

"Oh my God, Mom," I said with an exasperated sigh. "I sure hope they pay it back."

"I do too, honey," she replied quietly.

As I hung up I imagined her in her green leather chair, her hand worriedly swirling her cigarette in a vortex in her ashtray.

Mom called me again the next day. "You'll never guess who I heard from *today*,"

"I'm afraid to ask," I replied wearily.

"Noreen," Mom said drawing the name out much too long.

"Does she want money too? I'm sure you could get an extension on your credit with the bank."

"I guess I made the mistake of talking with her when Michael moved in, and now she thinks we're best friends. "Hey, Barb," Mom said, imitating Aunt Noreen's perky voice, "What's doin'?'" I remembered the voice all too clearly. "Listen," Mom continued imitating Noreen, "I heard you might have a vacancy over there, and I'm thinkin' you might want to save some money and have a roommate."

"*AAAAHHHHHH*!!!" I yelled. "The nerve!"

Mom laughed and gave a long, drawn-out "ooohhhh" before continuing. "I told her I didn't think it was a good idea and that there was too much water under the bridge. "Oh geez, Barb," Mom imitated my aunt again, "that was ages ago. Besides, this way, we can both save some money. Whaddya say?'"

I laughed again despite myself. Of course, she was going to let her move in. "Mom, promise me you'll make her pay rent."

"You bet I will. If Michael misses his credit card payment, at least I'll have the rent from Noreen to pay it. She's got a social security check every month, and I have the only key to the mailbox. I told her no drinking and no whining, and if she does either one, she's out."

"I'll help you remove her if she doesn't pay."

Aunt Noreen moved in a couple of days later with only a dresser and some clothes. After she was settled in, Mom called me from the phone in her bedroom. "At least, we won't have a lot of stuff to move if we have to get her out, Peg," she whispered.

* * *

June, 1988

George got the job. It was hard not to be excited for him as he danced me around the kitchen. I just wasn't thrilled for me. Not only would I be spending money I didn't have to fly down to see him, but I also had to find a cheaper place to live. I had used the bulk of money Paul had given me from the house to pay off my credit cards. Though I loved my work, I still wasn't making much money.

Shane, about to enter second grade, complained about the drives from San Ramon to The City. I couldn't blame him—after three years, they were wearing on me, too. With my new car phone and fax machine, I could easily correspond with clients no matter where I was. My dreams had been born in San Francisco, but they were part of me now. I could move wherever I liked.

Though I looked at several places in Oakland and Berkeley, they were all too expensive or run down. When a friend recommended some new apartments in San Ramon I reluctantly went to see them. They were spacious with a tennis court and pool. Living in San Ramon would save countless hours of driving. Besides, Shane would have friends to play with nearby. I moved in on July 1. On July 2, we invited Shane's friends over to our pool for his seventh birthday.

Flying high was great, but sometimes it was nice to just hang out by the pool.

* * *

July, 1988

Just after George moved to LA for his new job, the Chinese Chamber awarded us the contract for the Chinese New Year Parade. Though I'd have to do twice the work, it was worth it. I'd be immersed in marketing something I already loved—Chinese culture. I eagerly started putting together corporate sponsorship packages—including opportunities such as floats and specialty units, lion dancers and marching bands—and gathering a database of potential sponsors.

By that time, I had already tied together all the loose ends of my concert proposal for the project I called "War on AIDS" and sent a copy to Bill Graham. I was shocked when his office called to say he'd meet with me. His company had been involved with practically every concert I'd ever attended.

That day, I was ushered into a corner office upstairs. Though I expected a meeting with his assistant, instead it was Bill Graham, in jeans and rumpled shirt with rolled up sleeves, who strolled in. I stood to shake his hand but he waved at me to sit. I sat down on the edge of my seat.

He glanced at my proposal, which lay in front of him on his desk.

"Well, young lady, you've definitely got chutzpa." *Well, at least someone thinks I'm young.* His penetrating gaze under bushy eyebrows softened when he smiled. "You do know that we already have a concert planned?"

"I had no idea," I apologized.

"I lost a good friend to AIDS just last year. We've got to do *something* about this damn epidemic." I'd heard he could be ruthless, but, at that moment, he looked downright vulnerable.

I nodded. "My brother has AIDS."

"Look," his voice was gruff, "there's a group with Catholic Charities that's putting this thing together. I'll get you their number, and you give them a call."

I met with the group a couple of weeks later. By the end of July, they'd put me in on the front lines as the sponsorship and project coordinator.

* * *

August, 1988

Glenn was getting sicker. The AIDS drugs no longer made him feel better. They just kept him alive. His body temperature vacillated between extreme highs and lows. He was tired of sweats and shots and feeling miserable. He wanted to be done with it all and die. He stopped taking drugs and entered the hospice program at Kaiser. He still hadn't told Mom he had AIDS, no doubt in part because of Dad's recent death: always the protector.

"She's his mother. She has the right to know so she can say good-bye!" I said stridently to Pat and Sue, who sat with me in the hall of the hospital while Glenn's IV was being changed. It was hard enough for me to be missing out on half of Shane's life. I couldn't imagine the pain of losing my son without being able to say good-bye.

Sue put her hands to her mouth in thought.

"Do what you need to do, Peg," Pat said.

Later that evening, I stood at Mom's apartment door: Though the hallway had been painted and the carpeting replaced to justify higher rent, her door was still hollow plywood. I closed my eyes and rapped: another knock, another child.

Mom answered in robe and slippers. The A's game blasted from the television in the living room. Aunt Noreen's hearing wasn't good. "Egetha! Glad you stopped by, honey."

Aunt Noreen sprawled in the burnt orange chair, a plate of meat loaf and peas on a TV tray in front of her. Criss-cross bobby pins covered her head. "Hey, Peg!" she said boisterously chewing, "How 'bout those A's!"

I waved as Mom ushered me into her bedroom. We sat down on her bed.

"Mom, I just saw Glenn," I said, trying to find the right tone.

"How is that 'ole Grinchie?" Mom asked indulgently. "The little dickens hasn't called me in a while."

I willed her eyes to meet mine. "Not good, Mom."

"The meningitis *again*, Peg?" she asked. Her smile disappeared.

I blew air from my lips like from a deflating balloon and then clamped them shut as if, for an instant, weighing whether I should tell her. But she was his mother. She had a right to know. I tightened my fists to gather strength. "No, Mom. Glenn has AIDS."

Mom squeezed her eyes shut. Her body shuddered as she sighed. I held her shoulder to keep her from falling. When she opened her eyes, they held a calm sadness I'd never seen before. "Honey, should I call him and tell him that I know, and that it's okay? The last thing that poor baby needs is to be worried about what I'm thinking."

"I know he'll be angry with me for telling you, Mom, but I think you should go see him," I said taking her hand. I kneaded her fingers like clay as I said softly, "I don't think he's got much longer."

The tears stayed put in the corners of her eyes. She gave my hand a hard squeeze. "Thanks, honey, for letting me know."

Glenn glared at me the next day when I brought Mom to see him. He pulled himself up in bed with difficulty as he adjusted his oxygen mask. "Mom, I really don't feel too well," he said, lifting up the mask so she could hear him better.

Mom used her cool hand to smooth back the drenched hair on his brow. "Gosh, Grinchie, you coulda fooled *me*." They both laughed.

They sat quietly for a few minutes, and then Mom stood. She cupped Glenn's face in her hand as she gazed into his eyes. "You save a nice spot up there for your mother, honey. Tell Daddy to stay put until I get there."

"Will do," Glenn said with wet eyes. Behind the wet, his eyes twinkled.

* * *

The next day, I stopped by the hospital before flying down to see George in LA. Glenn would go soon. Losing him would be bad enough: I couldn't stay and watch him die.

Glenn was in a deep morphine-induced sleep when I arrived. I pulled a tape out of my purse and dropped it in the cassette player on the swivel table near his hospital bed and turned up the volume. Aretha Franklin's *Who's Zoomin Who* blared from the small speakers. Glenn and I both loved the song.

Sue ran in from the hall where she'd been talking quietly with her new partner, Marny. "Peg!" she said frowning as she turned the volume down. I knew it was inappropriate to blast music in the hospice ward, but this was Glenn, who'd always been the first one to turn up the volume on our favorite songs, and he was fading away. Maybe he'd be able to hear it in the netherworld he was occupying. I didn't care what the hospice workers thought. I wanted to see Glenn's body move and mouth grin one more time as he danced to the beat.

Sue, our family's self-appointed medical watchdog, sat down in the chair next to the hospital bed.

I stroked Glenn's arm. It felt cool. I ran my fingers through his hair. He didn't move. "How's he been?" I asked.

"The same: heavily medicated, sleeping most of the time. This morning his arms and legs started flailing as he struggled for air. Luckily the hospice nurse was here and gave him more medication."

"Where's Pat?" I asked.

"He went to have a cigarette." Sue adjusted Glenn's blanket.

"Sue ... I know I'm a coward. But I have to get out of here," I said

"I know you do," she said. "It's okay."

I cradled Glenn's hand. I tried but couldn't take a full breath. I looked at his graying face, his sunken cheeks. I kissed him on his sweat-drenched temple and whispered in his ear, "See ya later."

Sue and I hugged. "Say good-bye to Pat," I said, and zoomed out the door.

Within an hour, I was pushing my carry-on bag into the overhead compartment and dropping down in my seat. I leaned back hard, disappointed in myself for leaving the side of my dying brother. As the plane rose above the clouds, I looked out the window. I imagined Glenn laughing as he zoomed by in his big wooden school chair. Ever the teacher, he had always encouraged me to go after what I wanted in life, and to enjoy doing it.

I was glad to have the row to myself. I cried and shivered. Without Glenn, the world would be a cold, boring place.

Since George was at work, I used the key he'd given me to open the door of his apartment. I took off my shoes and climbed into the bed. Feeling cold to the bone, I pulled the blankets up under my chin. Life was nothing but a series of sad events. Nothing lasted forever, and the good things barely lasted any time at all. I wanted to sink down into darkness and never come back up.

The phone rang.

I'd given Sue George's number to call me when Glenn died. Though I wouldn't need to fly home for a funeral since he didn't want one, I still wanted to be told when it happened. The words, "Glenn's gone, Peg," rolled through my mind as the phone rang five … six … seven times. Maybe if I didn't answer it, it wouldn't be true.

I rolled over and picked up.

"Hello, Peg?" Odd … Sue's voice sounded almost cheerful.

"Sue," I whispered. "It's Glenn, isn't it?"

"Peg, there's someone here who wants to talk with you," Sue said.

"Honey," a gravelly voice said.

"Oh, my God!" I screamed as I bolted up, "Grinchie, is that you?"

"Who else did you suppose it would be?" he asked with a clipped laugh.

"*It's so good to hear your voice!*" I screeched in delight.

"I just had one more thing I wanted to say to you …" Glenn said with what sounded like a grin.

"Okay," I said, still incredulous.

His breathing was heavy on the other end. "Have fun."

I closed my eyes to savor his words.

"I will," I said, smiling so hard it hurt.

Glenn and Pat's voices were muffled in the background when Sue got back on the phone. "Thanks so much, Sue," I said, grateful down to my toes.

"Peg, he woke up and said he had to talk to you. Who were we to try and stop him?" she replied.

As with the elephant box he gave me when he left home so many years before, on his way out, Glenn had dropped a treasure in my lap.

After Sue and I said good-bye, I hung up the phone. An image of Glenn grinning while he danced popped into my head. He pointed at me. "You go, Pegs."

Glenn died early the next morning.

Chapter 27

❦

Portable City

September, 1988

Now that we weren't spending so much time driving back and forth to The City, I finally had the time to both provide for Shane's needs and have fun with him. We played baseball and soccer on the big lawn in front of my apartment. A never-ending game of Monopoly occupied a corner of my living room floor. Each night, curled up reading, we were transported to C.S. Lewis's mythical land of Narnia.

That fall, Shane entered third grade. As his subjects grew more challenging, it became obvious that he was struggling. He had a terrible time memorizing math facts and took hours to complete his homework. I thought he just wasn't trying. He came up with his own way of helping himself concentrate: he would pretend to open the top of his head to let all the frogs out. It was creative, and seemed to work, at least until the frogs returned.

When his teacher called after just a few weeks to say that she'd moved him "from the back of the class, to the middle, and finally right next to me in front of the class so he'll pay attention," I had him tested. He was diagnosed with Attention Deficit Disorder. Of course, I blamed the problem on Paul's genes. Mine were way too marvelous. Paul and I had always chalked up all the lost homework papers and books left at school to the confusion of coming from a broken family. But ironically enough, separated from each other, Paul and I had become a much more effective parenting team.

Unlike many people, I had no problem with my child taking Ritalin. I'd seen what the right drugs could do for my mother. Ritalin allowed Shane to finally keep up with the class.

On the days that Paul had Shane, I often worked eighteen to twenty hours. Though I'd already secured some sponsors for the Chinese New Year Parade, the AIDS benefit had added three new shows at three additional venues. As the project expanded, so did my job. To top things off, a colleague had recommended me to the Sierra Club, and I agreed to produce a Founder's event for them. Though I was now earning really good money, I didn't want to turn anything down: I never knew when there might be a downturn in demand for my services.

I lost track of time as I made endless lists of "Things to Do," and "People to Call." Finally, neck cramped and contacts stuck to my eyes, I turned off my computer and fell into bed. How long could I keep up this pace?

* * *

January, 1989

In late January, Bonnie and I planned to meet for lunch at her office in Alameda. I found a parking space in the lot where I'd been so many times before and reached into the backseat to get my purse. When I faced forward, nothing looked familiar.

Was I in San Francisco for a meeting? I stared at the mobile phone mounted on my console. When I faced forward, the configuration of the radio knobs below the air-conditioner, the coffee mug on the floor, the small tissue package shoved in the cup holder were unfamiliar: Was I sitting in someone else's car? I covered my eyes with my hands as my heart pounded. How could that be possible? Whose was that? *Oh God, where in the hell am I?* I took a deep breath. *Don't panic.*

I got out of the car and walked to the nearest building. A woman at the security desk in the lobby asked, "Can I help you?"

I couldn't say. I wasn't sure why I was there.

"Not just yet," I said, forcing a smile. There, next to the elevator, was a sign. 'Harbor Bay Company,' it read. Harbor Bay ... Harbor Bay ... I closed my eyes to concentrate. *Good Lord.* Other people worried about genetic defects like heart disease or high cholesterol. Lucky me: my body got to choose between Alzheimer's and mental illness—those marvelous genes again.

The elevator opened. A woman walked toward me. "Bonnie!" I cried out in relief.

"Peg, are you okay?"

She waved at the person at the front desk, who must have called to see if anyone was waiting for a visitor.

"I know her," she said to the woman.

"Bon ..." I said, trying to swallow over the lump in my throat. "I didn't know where I was. I didn't recognize anything ... I've been here so many times, and I didn't recognize ..." Bonnie hugged me. "... anything. I'm so glad you came."

"Peg," Bon said taking my arm, "let's forget lunch. Wanna just take a walk?"

As we strolled I poured out my story of long working hours, project deadlines and demands, and my fears that I wasn't going to be able to get everything done.

Bon raised her eyebrows. "Let me come over and help you, Peg. I'm in marketing—I'm sure there are some things I can do."

"Bon," I asked looking into her eyes so that I could see the truth, "do you think I'm losing my mind?"

Bonnie gripped my arm reassuringly. "No, Peg. I think you're just too stubborn to ask for help. Have you forgotten that you lost two very important people in your life within the past twelve months? Not to mention the fact that you've recently moved, you've been separated first from your husband, and now, your boyfriend, and you've taken on three huge events?"

I laughed. "Okay, I'm sounding pathetic enough. Please, no more."

That weekend, Bon helped me get through a huge pile of work I hadn't had time to tackle.

Bon's intervention was just the lift I needed to get through the events of the next few months. In early February, the Sierra Club Founder's event went so smoothly that I found myself making jokes with the guests as I sat with them at dinner. I loved my job!

George sat next to me on the bleachers a week later at the Chinese New Year Parade, while Paul and Shane sat a few rows behind us. Loud drums and cymbals accompanied the vibrantly colorful groups of fluffy lion dancers that stopped to perform in front of us. I turned to watch Shane, who had come down near me to try and touch the playful lions as they opened their mouths and wagged their tails like giant cuddly toys.

Massive butterflies with wings outlined in chaser lights floated toward us down the street. "Here comes Southwest Airlines' float!" I said excitedly to George. They were one of my sponsors. The float was gorgeous!

I turned around and pointed to Paul at the float just as thousands of firecrackers made a deafening explosion. We laughed as we covered our ears.

When the parade was over, I hugged Shane and watched as he and Paul walked back to their car. For a second, I wished I was going with them.

Instead, I walked with George back to mine.

"Congratulations, girlfriend, on another successful event." I liked the sound of "successful." But somehow, my relationship with George had not progressed like the rest of my life.

By May, the AIDS benefit, renamed *In Concert Against AIDS*, had grown to include many AIDS organizations, celebrities, and a long list of events. Linda Ronstadt did a show at the Gift Center and Huey Lewis and the News performed at Slim's Nightclub. The Grateful Dead, Joe Satriani, Los Lobos, John Fogerty, and Tracy Chapman headlined a rock show at the Coliseum, while Bob "Bobcat" Goldthwaite and Marga Gomez joined other comedians at the Warfield. A cabaret show, gospel show, and a giant Conga line in the Mission rounded out the line-up of events. Major sports figures did PSAs to raise AIDS awareness. Though Glenn was gone, I hoped the money raised would keep others with AIDS alive until there was a cure.

* * *

September, 1989

For my thirty-fifth birthday, George rented a cottage on Catalina Island. We took a tour of the Avalon Ballroom, then strolled hand-in-hand along the curved veranda. We stopped and leaned up against the railing to look out to blue sea past the boats anchored in the harbor. A row of seagulls eyed us from a railing.

"We could be married here," George said.

I was shocked. We'd never talked of marriage before. Why would he mention it now? If anything, we'd grown apart.

I looked into his eyes. They twinkled like the first time we met across a board room table and as they had again when hand-in-hand, we'd stood watching the fireworks we'd planned explode over the Bay Bridge. In the past, the you-know-you-love-me grin he wore now would have reached out and pulled me in, because he was right. But now I stayed put. "Geo, I'm not ready to get married."

His dark hair glistened in the sun as his head bowed. When he looked up, his blue eyes were flat. "If you're not ready now, when will you ever be?" he asked.

Images raced through my head: George wearing a rainbow Mohawk wig and fatigues, body twisting and feet pounding as he danced with me: a conehead prom queen; a late night event strategy session at our kitchen table; a screaming match over how Shane was out of control; tearful good-byes at LAX, jubilant reunions at Oakland airport; arguments over whose turn it was to fly. I was silent.

"Well, I guess that's my answer," he said, his mouth twisting. "Why even continue seeing each other if nothing is going to come of it?" he asked.

"Maybe we should start dating other people," I said, looking away.

Though neither one of us said so, it was clear to me that the relationship we'd had was over.

* * *

October 17, 1989

With a magnitude of 7.1, the Loma Prieta earthquake hit at 5:04 p.m. It lasted fifteen to twenty seconds, during which the floor of my second story apartment wobbled and Shane and I stood together in a doorway while I pretended it was a big adventure. It was the biggest quake since 1906.

As I swept up the glass in the kitchen, the living room television came back on. "This just in ... the Bay Bridge has suffered some serious damage from the earthquake ..." On the screen, a span of the top deck of the Bay Bridge hung at an angle blocking the lower deck. One car had driven off the edge of the gap, crashing onto the lower deck killing the driver. *Good God, it ripped apart the bridge?* What other damage did it do?

An image of a collapsed portion of freeway took the place of the ruined bridge. The anchor intoned, "A portion of the Cypress Freeway has collapsed. It's feared that as many as fifty people are trapped in their cars underneath ..."

My hand went to my mouth. Paul took the Cypress Freeway on his way home from work. I glanced in at Shane watching television on my bed. *Paul!* I clasped my hands. *Please God, let him be okay.* Tragically, forty-two people had died.

Fifteen minutes later, there was a knock at my door. I went to answer ... It was Paul! I threw my arms around him and held him tight. "I was so worried about you," I said anxiously.

"Wow!" he said. "What a welcome!"

Shane ran to give Paul a hug.

"Did you hear what happened to the bridge?" I asked.

"I heard: I was driving on the freeway and all of a sudden it felt like I had a blowout. I pulled off onto the shoulder at the same time as a bunch of other people. We were all walking around our cars looking at our tires."

We laughed.

"So what made you come by?" I asked.

Peggy Kennedy

"Once I turned on the radio and heard it was an earthquake, I wanted to make sure you guys were okay."

"You feel like staying for spaghetti?" I asked brightly.

"Sure, it's my favorite," he said with a smile.

"I know." I grinned.

My bridge had collapsed. Luckily, I'd already carried my city with me to the other side.

Chapter 28

⚜

A Beautiful Sight

Six months later

As I waited with Shane for Paul to answer the door, I looked around the porch of my old house in San Ramon: new bench, new paint, and new half-circle window above the front door. Paul had kept the place in nice shape. I knocked again. I was dropping Shane off before leaving for a three-day sponsorship conference in Chicago. Paul was living alone now that Debbie had moved out. He opened the door, and Shane bolted past him up the stairs to the toys in his room.

"Wanna come in?" Paul asked.

"No, I gotta go," I said although part of me wanted to stay. "I'm running late, as usual."

Paul handed me an envelope. "Here's some reading material for the plane." By the look in his eyes, it wasn't your average reading material.

I raised my eyebrows. "Can you give me a hint?"

"No. Just one thing, if you read it and you don't like what it says, pretend you never saw it, okay?"

He hadn't acted like this since seventh grade. My heart raced. I thought my anxiety of losing him during the earthquake had been just the fear of losing a good friend. But now, I was blushing.

Back at my apartment, I handed my bag to the Airporter van driver and climbed in to the backseat. Paul's envelope held a card with a photo of a boy and girl holding hands. Tears formed in my eyes. Someone jostled me as they sat down. I opened it. Paul's handwriting was neater than usual.

"Dear Peg: I was scared to death to give this to you, but felt like I had to take the chance, so here goes. I understand now what you meant when you told me five years ago that you weren't leaving me to have a relationship with someone else, but because you needed to rediscover who you were." Without warning, my tears started to fall. "I'm so proud of everything that you've accomplished since you left! It's hard to believe that you've done so many great things; but then, I shouldn't be surprised." The tears flowed. The woman next to me stared, but I didn't care. "Finally, I think I've met someone through this dating service that I could get serious with." My hand went to my mouth. "But I don't want to pursue it if there's a chance for you and me to get back together. Although it might seem like a long shot to you, it's what I've wanted all along. Think about it.

Love, Paul."

My shoulders shook as I sobbed. Everyone in the van turned to stare. I found an old tissue in my purse and held it to my nose. *I was still in love with him!*

I called Paul from the hotel, but when he answered, I couldn't make any words come out. Somehow, he knew it was me. "Peg?" he asked.

"Uh-huh."

"You read the letter?"

"Uh-huh." I sniffed.

"Do you hate me?" he asked quietly.

"No," I squeaked out.

"Could we try again?" he asked fearlessly.

"I don't know," I managed to get out.

"Are you willing to try?" his voice was hopeful.

I sighed heavily. "I'm scared. I don't want to be who I was. I like who I am now."

"I like who you are now too," he said gently.

"Are you sure about that?" I asked. "I'm not the shy, innocent girl you used to love. I'm stubborn, and pushy, and I like getting my own way."

"I've noticed," he said laughing.

"What about Shane?" I asked, suddenly really considering the possibility. "Do we really want to put him through this again? What if it doesn't work and we split up again? He'd be devastated!"

"But what if it does work out? He'd be pretty excited, wouldn't he? Paul asked, undaunted.

I laughed. "Yep, he would."

"Maybe we just don't tell him until we know if it's going to work," Paul said.

"But how do we know if it's going to work?" I asked, desperately wanting to know for myself if it could. Just thinking about trying was making me exhausted.

"We'll figure that part out later," he said.

I laughed nervously. "Let's talk about it when I get back in a few days," I said.

"That's great!" he exclaimed. "Peg?" he asked in a soft voice I remembered from tender moments past.

"Yeah?" I asked, feeling just inches away from him on my parents' front porch.

"Thanks for calling." He said, as though squeezing my hand tight.

"Thanks for the card." I answered, squeezing back. When I hung up the phone, I shook my head in disbelief.

* * *

"If we're gonna try this, we have to see a therapist first," I said to Paul when I picked up Shane after my trip. "Do you want to pick someone?"

"I'm fine with whoever you pick," he said.

"Man or woman?"

"Woman. The last male therapist I saw called me a 'master manipulator.' He was probably right, but a woman would have said it in a much nicer way," he laughed.

It was good to hear him talk about his shortcomings without being defensive. I'd make the effort to let my defenses down too.

A couple of weeks later, Paul and I sat across from a cordial, dark-haired woman in a pantsuit. "Why would you each be better off together than alone?' she asked, looking from me to Paul.

"Now that I'm doing what I love, I'm happier. I think I can bring more to a relationship," I answered. *Fullness from fullness.*

The counselor smiled and looked at Paul. "How about you, Paul? Do you feel that you'd be better off with Peggy than alone?"

Paul shrugged. "I've never stopped loving her. How could I not be better off with her?"

I studied him. His laugh lines made his eyes seem bluer. His nose and chin had taken on a chiseled look. It was impossible, but true: with age, Paul had become even more handsome.

The counselor's gaze was intent on Paul, "Are you frightened that she might leave you again?"

Surprised by her directness, Paul lifted his eyebrows. "A little," he said, pursing his lips and nodding. The thumb from one hand rubbed the other nervously.

We looked at each other.

The counselor tipped her head toward me. "How would you answer that question?"

I didn't hesitate. "I know I'm okay on my own. I can take care of myself. I'm here because I want to be. I realize that if we get back together again, it will take some time for him to trust me."

After the session, when our hands touched as we walked down the stairs, I had a tingling sensation I hadn't felt in years. When we stopped in front of my car, I felt like we were back in eighth grade. Was he going to kiss me? He leaned closer. I did, too. As we brushed lips, I inhaled his fragrance. *Pull me in.*

* * *

July, 1990

Over the next couple of months, our dates became more frequent than our counseling sessions. By July, we were talking about moving back in together. The time had come to let Shane know what was up. For the first few years after our break up, Shane had begged us to get back together again. Now, it seemed, he had resigned himself to the fact that it would never happen. Now we were going to tell him that we'd changed our minds?

Paul invited me over to the house for Shane's birthday. As Paul carried the cake with nine candles to the table, Paul and I sang my family's birthday song:

"Today is a birthday
I wonder for whom ...

I know it's for someone ...
Who's right in this room ..."

Shane closed his eyes, made a wish, and blew out the candles.
"Honey, what was your wish?" I asked.
"If I tell you, it won't come true," he answered.
I took a deep breath. "What if we told you that Dad and I are thinking about getting back together?" I asked hopefully.
The clock ticked on the oven. Shane's expression fell. *Oh no.*
Shane shrugged. He stood up. "I'll be upstairs," he said quietly.
We let him go.
I looked at Paul anxiously.
"Let's see what he says after he's had a chance to think about it," Paul said.
Thirty minutes later, Shane's bedroom door opened and footsteps came down the stairs. Paul and I watched apprehensively as he approached.
Shane stopped at the door that adjoined the foyer to the kitchen and leaned his body in. "Can I ask you guys a question?" he asked seriously.
"Sure," Paul and I both replied.
He grinned with all his front teeth. "Does this mean I won't be able to get away with anything anymore?"
I called Mom that night to share the good news. I'd avoided telling her that Paul and I were dating: I hadn't wanted her to get her hopes up.
"Mom, are you sitting down?" I asked.
"Oh, Peg, honey, I'm so glad you called. Noreen has had a fever all day and it just shot up to a hundred and three. She's got a terrible cough. Do you think we could take her to Emergency?"
My news could wait. "Sure, Mom, I'll be there as soon as I can."
When I arrived, Aunt Noreen was coughing as Mom bundled her up in a blanket to go outside. Mom was big on blankets for

fevers. "Barb, I'm burnin' up, for Chrissakes," Aunt Noreen said as she threw the blanket to the floor.

Mom rolled her eyes. "Okay, we'll just bring it with us." She threw the blanket over her arm.

We waited in the Emergency waiting room for quite awhile before a nurse approached Mom. "Is Noreen Wall your sister?"

"Yes," Mom said apprehensively.

"She's got double pneumonia. We're going to have to admit her."

On the way back to her apartment, Mom dabbed her eyes. "Double pneumonia," she said sniffing as she shook her head. "Noreen is not strong enough to shake that off."

"I'm sorry, Mom," I said patting her hand.

Mom sighed. "She's a piece of work, that one, but she's still my sister."

We drove in silence until we reached her apartment. When I pulled into her parking space, she put her hand on my leg. "Now what was it you wanted to tell me, Egetha?"

I'd almost forgotten. I smiled. "I think Paul and I are getting back together."

I expected her to jump out of her seat in delight. Instead, she said, "You know, honey, I'd like nothing better than to see the two of you together again. I adore Paul. But more than anything, I want you to be happy."

"I *am* happy, Mom." I nodded.

She obviously saw it on my face. "In that case, I'm ecstatic!" she said with a big smile.

Mom called me one morning a week later, crying. "Aunt Noreen passed away last night, honey."

"I'm so sorry, Mom."

"Me, too, honey." She sighed and took a drag off her cigarette. As she exhaled, she said: "I'll bet your father's standing at the pearly gates with a fire hose so she can't come in."

* * *

September, 1990

Paul and I pulled everything out of all the closets in the house to prepare for the painters and carpet installers. I'd decided it was only fair that I reinvest the money Paul had given me from the equity into updating the house. Luckily, I'd been able to earn and save the amount of money he'd originally given me from the house, and more. By investing in the house, I was showing Paul that I intended to stay, sharing responsibilities equally. Besides, there was no way I wanted to move back in with everything the same as it had been.

When the workers were finished, I set up my work space with computer, printer, fax, and copier in the downstairs bedroom. When I was done, I gazed out the window. Giant laurel and oak trees formed a lush wall along the creek. Rays of sunlight peered through the branches. The leaves on the trees were blowing gently.

It was a beautiful sight.

Chapter 29

~∂\~

Fairy Dust

One year later

The bargains on coffee, pastries, cigarettes, and Metamucil at Longs Drugs still beckoned my mother even after Dad died. So every other Tuesday after I took her to get her Lithium shot, Mom and I trolled the store's aisles for the catch of the day. Somewhere between the end of aisle display of peanut butter and aisle of children's puzzles and toys, Mom grabbed my arm firmly. Before I knew what was happening, she passed out. When the store manager and I couldn't revive her, he called an ambulance. I rode with her to the hospital. "Her blood pressure is near zero," one of the paramedics said to the other.

"*Zero?*" I asked, alarmed.

"Yes, Ma'am," he answered quickly. At the hospital, they rolled her into intensive care. I called Pat and Sue.

Over the next few days, the three of us took turns standing watch while Mom slept motionless. Pat was sitting next to her when, on the fourth day, she opened her eyes.

He took her hand. "Well, hello, Mother," he said, grinning.

"How in the world did I get *here?*" she asked.

"I don't know, Mom," Pat said laughing, "Peg says you went on a wild shopping spree at Longs. They felt that the only way to stop you was to bring you here."

Mom giggled and raised her eyebrows like Mother Grinch. "Gosh, did I get anything good?"

They moved Mom out of intensive care that afternoon. During our visit to Mom's room the next day, Sue turned on the television. "A fire is spreading dangerously through the Oakland Hills. The fire department is urging any homeowners in these areas to evacuate their homes immediately." On the screen was a list of the neighborhoods in danger.

"Oh my God!" Sue said jumping up. "That's near Marny's house! I've got to go!" she grabbed her purse and was gone in a flash.

Later that afternoon, Mom's doctor came in. "Barbara, it looks like you're doing much better. We've run some tests, and think this happened because of all the antipsychotic drugs you're taken over the years. We're going to send you home tomorrow. Try to get a little exercise: you need to build up your strength again. And by all means, quit smoking!"

"Yes, doctor," Mom said angelically, eager as always, to please those in charge.

"She shouldn't be on her own yet," Patrick said to me in the hallway.

"I'll take her to my house," I said.

I prepared the guest room upstairs for Mom, but climbing up the stairs was difficult.

"Honey, how 'bout if I just sleep on the couch in the family room?" she asked. "That way, I won't miss anything," she added mischievously.

The next morning, Mom lay sleeping under a bundle of blankets on the couch as I tiptoed by on my way to my office to start work.

"Hi, Egetha," she whispered.

"Hi, Mom," I whispered back. "Wanna cup of coffee?"

"Sure," she smiled. Of course she did. What a question!

I poured a cup, stirred in two teaspoonfuls of sugar and brought it to her. She took a sip. "Ahhh, that's good, Peg."

I sat down on the coffee table next to her. We sipped quietly for a couple of minutes. Finally, Mom broke the silence. "Honey, we're dropping like flies."

I almost spit out my coffee. Our eyes met. Her laugh came from deep in the belly where dark Irish humor lurks until just the right moment.

Her laugh was infectious. Soon, we were bending over, trying to catch our breath with wet eyes and running noses. God's giant flyswatter had hit our family again and again, and there wasn't a damn thing we could do. She would most likely get the next swat. But life was an illusion. Love was the real living.

A few days later, I found some cigarette butts hidden in the bushes: Mom had started smoking again. I confronted her later that day. "Mom, the doctor said you're not supposed to be smoking."

"Oh, honey," Mom's voice, spiraling lower, had accepted defeat, "I've tried to quit before. I just can't."

I threw up my hands and walked away.

The next day, Mom helped me fold the laundry. After dinner that night, she insisted on doing the dishes. Before I headed up to bed, I turned off the light over the stove in the kitchen and walked to the couch to give her a kiss goodnight.

She pushed herself up onto her elbow. "Honey, I think I'm ready to move back to my apartment."

I was alarmed. "Mom, are you sure you're feeling up to it? You've been out of the hospital less than a week."

"Yes, I'm sure," she said, patting my leg reassuringly. "I'm feeling much better now," she added.

I moved her back to her apartment the next day. After we settled her back in, she made a list of groceries that she needed at the store. When I returned from shopping, a cigarette burned in the ashtray next to her green leather chair.

* * *

Four months later

A friend of Patrick's recommended me to a company providing sponsor hospitality at the upcoming Summer Olympic Games. Though I was thrilled when I got a letter offering me a job in Barcelona, a knot formed in my stomach. Paul wouldn't want me to go.

That night at dinner, I broke the news. "I got a letter today from a company asking me to work at the Barcelona Olympics this summer." I smiled hopefully.

"Where's Barcelona?" Shane asked.

I gladly turned to face Shane. "It's in northern Spain, honey."

"For how long?" Paul asked.

"I'd be gone a month," I said squirming.

"Can we come?" Shane asked.

"Yeah," Paul smiled, "Can we come?"

I was shocked. "Really?"

"Sure!" Paul said. "Maybe we could travel for a while around Europe and end up in Barcelona to drop you off when you start work." Paul had never wanted to travel long distances before.

"Great idea!" I said excitedly. "You really would?" I beamed.

* * *

February, 1992

Mom was crying on the phone. My heart beat faster. The last time I heard her cry was when Aunt Noreen died.

"Mom, what's wrong?" I asked, filling with panic.

"Peg, I'm really sick. I've been throwing up all night. I'm scared, honey. What I'm throwing up is brown. I think it might be blood." She'd seemed fine two days before when I'd taken her to get her Lithium shot. How could she get so sick so fast?

Shane was in school. "I'll be right there, Mom." I said.

The front door was unlocked, so I walked in. Her room smelled like a rodent had died in the wall. Mom lay exhausted against the headboard, her hair soaked and her nightgown covered with brown stains. The garbage can that was normally filled with old bills and receipts under her desk was next to her bed and full of some thick, brown fluff. It had the grainy consistency of Metamucil.

She didn't smile as I gave her a hug.

"Mom, we need to get you to the hospital," I said.

She started to cry again. "No, Peg," she sobbed. "Please don't take me there. I may never come home. They'll poke me and take my blood all day long. I hate that place."

I sat down on her bed and held her hand. I started to cry too. We sat there, holding hands, both of us crying.

Finally, Mom sighed heavily. "Okay, Peg, if you say so. Help me get ready."

Mom was taken into intensive care. Patrick flew out and Sue drove down. At the hospital, nurses poked Mom with needles and took her blood just as she'd expected. They ran tests. She was miserable. After a few days, she fell into a deep sleep. Although she squeezed our hands when we talked to her, she was otherwise unresponsive.

Pat had to go back to New York to finish a project. "I should be back next week, Peg," he said reluctantly. "Call me if I need to come sooner," he said.

Sue and I talked with Mom's doctor in her room the following day. "Your mother has advanced colon cancer. We could try to treat it, but I don't think it would help. We caught it too late."

I went into the corridor to be alone. It was too soon. She was only sixty-five.

When I came back in, wiping my face, Mom stirred and Sue took her hand. She leaned down next to her ear. "Mom, can you hear me?" she asked.

Mom nodded.

"The doctor just told us you have colon cancer. They don't recommend treatment."

Mom pressed her lips against each other and then released a couple of times as though trying to speak. Finally, she said faintly. "Now I can go." Over the next few days, she slept peacefully. Sometimes, she smiled. I couldn't help but think she was seeing Glenn and Dad and Joan again. A day or two later, I got the call.

All of the information we needed to make her funeral arrangements was in a neatly written note on her desk.

Pat arrived from New York the day after Mom died. He, Sue, and I made a trip to the mortuary to pick out a cushy pink coffin and to the florist to have them make up a spray of pink rosebuds to lie on top. We unanimously agreed on the words to be etched on her headstone:

BARBARA JANE KENNEDY
NOVEMBER 13, 1926–FEBRUARY 27, 1992
WONDERFUL MOTHER

* * *

Epilogue

⚜

Happily Ever After

Paul and I have moved from the house that backed up to a creek to a house on a hill with a view of Mount Diablo. Our son Shane lives in San Francisco in an apartment with a view of the lights on the Bay Bridge.

After five years of being back together, Paul and I had another baby and named him Blake. When he was four, Blake turned to face me as he lay on my lap on the couch and said matter-of-factly, "You know, Mommy, I'm not your baby, you're really mine." I laughed. I could see Mom pushing Dad and Glenn out of the way for the chance to come back. But I filed it away, knowing Blake, like Shane, will learn to love and be whoever he needs to be.

After twenty years, I'm still enjoying developing sponsorship for the Southwest Airlines Chinese New Year Parade, hoping that I'm helping to create something memorable for the hundreds of thousands of people that attend each year.

At this point, there are two things I know for sure:

The truth *is* right where I am.

And sometimes, good things can last and last. And last.

Printed in the United States
214817BV00002B/9/P

9 781440 126123